From Our Hearts to Yours

Why I Would Not Trade A Moment Of My Grief For A Life Less Loved

Pam Eade

"I loved *From Our Hearts to Yours* by Pam Eade. From the first page, I was totally engrossed. By the time I had finished, I had cried tears of pain for myself, for my mum, for my dad, and especially for Pam and Don. If you have gone through or are still going through the grief of losing a loved one, *From Our Hearts To Yours* will be an invaluable tool to help you move through the grief to find peace in your heart."

Rae Antony

"My husband of 38 years died suddenly from cardiac arrest 18 months ago without warning or any prior health issues. I plummeted into the darkest, deepest abyss of grief. I wanted to no longer exist. A friend encouraged me to read Pam's story. Through her words, I found something to cling on to. I found comfort in knowing there is someone who feels all the emotions I do and who understands my desperation. I am so grateful I was given these pages to read in my darkest hours!

Thank you, Pam."

Ellen Naumann

"I would love to thank you for bringing your book into my life. The timing was divine. As you know, my dad is really unwell and coming to the end of his life. It's tough to feel it coming and that time is nearing. This is really the first time I have been and will be confronted with the passing of a loved one. I feel that your book has already helped me immensely in this process of healing and that it will continue to, after my dad has chosen his final day. Thank you, Pam."

Emily Gowor

From Our Hearts to Yours: Why I would not trade a moment of my grief for a life less loved © Pam Eade 2022

The moral rights of Pam Eade to be identified as the author of this work have been asserted in accordance with the Copyright Act 1968.

First published in Australia 2022 by Pam Eade

ISBN 978-0-6452909-0-5

All rights reserved. No part of this publication may be reproduced or transmitted by any means, electronic, photocopying or otherwise, without prior written permission of the author.

Disclaimer

All the information, techniques, skills and concepts contained within this publication are of the nature of general comment only and are not in any way recommended as individual advice. The intent is to offer a variety of information to provide a wider range of choices now and in the future, recognising that we all have widely diverse circumstances and viewpoints. Should any reader choose to make use of the information herein, this is their decision, and the author and publisher/s do not assume any responsibilities whatsoever under any conditions or circumstances. The author does not take responsibility for the business, financial, personal or other success, results or fulfilment upon the readers' decision to use this information. It is recommended that the reader obtain their own independent advice.

This book is dedicated to:

Don Eade, the love of my life and semi-silent co-author.
He is more than my partner; he is a part of me.
Without him, this book could not have been written.

The front-page design was created by our son, Harley.

The photo, taken in 1996, simply vibrates with the deep love we had for each other.

The night sky image is significant in that it is the actual sky when and where Don and I first met - to be precise 7pm on Friday 23/5/1980 at the Grand Hotel, Palmerston North, New Zealand.

40.3581°S175.6103°E

Thanks to www.create.thenightsky.com for making it possible to access this image.

Contents

Introduction 1

PART I: "I can't believe you left me!" 7

   1: The characters are real characters.................... 11

   2: The beginning of the end.................................. 17

   3: But *I* wasn't ready... 29

   4: You are who you think you are 37

   5: "When you die..." 43

PART II: Looking for Don 47

   6: Not just my partner but a part of me................ 51

   7: Second message was classic Don – he's back!.. 59

   8: Can crying cause dehydration?......................... 67

   9: How I survived the funeral 71

   10: The end of the worst year ever! 79

   11: "Don, we need to talk" 87

   12: New Year's resolution – just survive............. 105

   13: Grief is love! 115

   14: "If I write down my thoughts, will I sound crazy?" 121

15: The much-anticipated talk with Don 133

16: I'm looking for peace but only finding pieces 153

17: Love knows no boundaries 163

18: "I understand" 169

19: Stick didn't work? Put carrots in the future.................. 179

20: Carrot number two is a real trip! 193

21: Twelve months – focus on the life, not the death 205

22: "What! How can you have left me again?" 213

23: It's clearer to see where I am now! 219

24: "OMG Don, did you just make me laugh?" 227

25: Third time is a charm... 233

26: Guiding me with clarity 249

27: "Really, it's been two years already!" 261

28: I'm not done yet, there's more... 267

29: How does this story end? 277

PART III: Survival toolkit – self-care in progress.................... 281

30: Self-care – where do I start? 287

31: You are who you think you are – still 315

Conclusion: from our hearts to yours 323

Resources that have helped shape my views.......................... 331

Acknowledgments 334

If love could have saved you, you would have lived forever.

Unknown

Introduction

"*L*ove you Pam," Don says as he rolls over to go to sleep. "Love you Don," I say. Words said from the heart. Four hours later Don died in his sleep. That was it. In a heartbeat I lost my husband of 37 years. I was devastated! Lucky for me he didn't go far. He was there to guide me through my grief, show me what life and death really is and help the words flow so this book could be in your hands.

I understand that if you were drawn to this book, you are probably experiencing or anticipating a loss or, if you're lucky, you are just curious.

My original intention, in writing about my experience, was to offer some form of comfort to those suffering the loss of a significant person in their life, as I have.

But really, it may provide some help for those whose death is considered pending and those who fear death, because, as they say, none of us get out of here alive, and we really don't know when we, or a loved one, will go.

When you feel down or sick, who do you turn to? Who always provides comfort or is overjoyed with your triumphs? Who knows when the little things are your big things? Who has more faith in you than you sometimes have in yourself? This is the person I lost. In my case it was my husband; for a friend, it was her mother, for another, her daughter was her 'soulmate' and for another it was her dog. It is about losing the most precious companion in your life, whoever they are.

Whatever your situation, I have written my story from my heart with the intent that people can take what they want from it. Relax, there's no test at the end and certainly no judgement. Maybe some quiet contemplation, *on your story*. I believe I suffered enough for everyone, but also understand that only I know my pain, and I do not want to assume to know yours.

From an early age we are taught to only show or express a 'socially acceptable' level of emotion. In my view this has caused so much more pain and suffering in the world than if we expressed ourselves honestly and without fear of judgement (this is not a free ride to hurting others though). Grief hurts! I have borne my soul in this book. My experience and therefore my story to begin with are raw, that's just reality. But there is no light without dark, they coexist, so although the dark appears absolute, the presence of light will eventually shine through.

If it gives you any comfort, I can confirm that I did, in fact, survive the most devastating loss and, as a bonus, I have no fear of death and instead have a new appreciation of life. If my story can help you in any way, then it has served its only purpose.

From my perspective, we appear to have no say in who we love and the intensity of it. Before I lost my husband, I had lost two sets of grandparents, my husband's parents, two young cousins, a work colleague and Ralph, our beloved dog. Without taking anything away from these wonderful people, I grieved for our dog, Ralph, with unparalleled intensity. My husband and children were also devastated. Our hearts broke. But that was nothing compared to the grief of losing my husband and life partner, Don. Absolutely nothing could have prepared me for the intensity of the pain.

My husband went *before* people we knew who were 'at death's door' or 'on borrowed time'. I, however, have been told that I won't be joining Don for 'a long time yet'. And, surprisingly, when given that advice, I considered it bad news. So, although this is my story of surviving intense grief, it is also Don's story of 'going home' (his words) and how my eyes were opened to a new appreciation of life and death. I no longer fear death because I know enough about what to expect.

I am not trained in grief counselling; that is not what this book is about. This is my story and Don's story.

I met my husband when I was just eighteen, before I had really experienced any life. He took me on an amazing journey, then, in the blink of an eye, we'd had thirty-seven wonderful years together and he died suddenly. I wasn't ready. I was devastated.

From birth, our mortality, and the mortality of those around us, is a given. We can't help but be touched by death. In my experience, most losses are 'manageable'; we get through okay. But we are so ill-prepared for the emotional fallout from the death of a most treasured loved one, and it is not even close to being manageable.

People die every minute of every day, and this must leave a staggering number of people in the world suffering from grief. So, why aren't we experts at this by now? Dammit!

Regardless, we experience grief in varying degrees, and my personal experience with my deepest loss is that absolutely nothing can prepare you for how you will feel. Don and I both knew early in our relationship that the greatest challenge we would *ever* face in life would be the loss of each other. I understood this but without any concept of the magnitude of what that experience would be.

Knowing it and being prepared for it are worlds apart. There is no possible preparation. It would be like bracing for the impact of a freight train. Like so many people, I suppose, I repeatedly asked myself how I was going to survive my loss. If you can't prepare, then there is only one alternative: managing as best you can after the fact and, ironically, when you are least equipped to do so.

It becomes an exercise in survival, and whether you think you can or know you don't want to, you will survive this purely because continuing to breathe is one of our basic instincts.

As I explore in Part II, the biggest and most unexpected aftershocks from losing my husband was that I found I didn't just lose him, I also lost 'us', and I lost me as well. The hardest loss to accept and understand was losing myself. I didn't recognise myself because I was forever changed from that day. I needed to stop trying to get back to the past me and start supporting this new me, who was a stranger.

So, how do you survive? Any number of people will tell you what to do. Unfortunately, the advice given to me from well-intentioned people who had experienced loss was actually detrimental to my mental state and in the end had no bearing on my reality. I came to realise that the advice was most often a conversation filler, a well-intentioned attempt on their part to provide 'spur of the moment' comfort. We've all done it, me included.

Viewing my husband's death through others' advice, I thought I must be doing everything wrong. People were especially wrong on the timeframes, which left me feeling weak and stupid. How could I be failing at grief? I was told that the first three months are the worst, but they were actually easier as I was in shock. I was told the first of every previously shared experience is the worst; actually, the second and third times were worse depending on the event. And after 4 years, December and Christmas is still a time I suffer through. I was told the first year is the worst. In the first year I focused on getting through, whereas in the second year, reality was a bitch. I was told it gets easier. It took me two years before it became easier to live on my own. Why was it not happening like people said it would? Because my experience wasn't theirs. All the events that led to the moment my best friend and husband died were unique to me/us.

I have come to realise that measuring healing in time is as accurate as 'how long is a piece of string'. Don gave me some wise words on this when he said, "It's about the heart; it's got nothing to do with time." So, now, when I continue to experience pain, I don't scold myself on where I *should* be at this time, and instead I say, "It's okay, it's as it should be because it's love."

Grief is personal. It was a long time before I understood that *I* needed to own my grief, 100 percent. *I* needed to work out how I would survive a life that I suddenly had no control over and didn't want.

The two absolute truths that sustained me during my grieving period that exceeded all timeframe expectations were:

Grief is love and

Love never dies.

Don and I loved each other intensely to the 'end'. A love that was strong and felt like it had a life of its own. In reality, love is abstract, it's a vibration, it's not reliant on the physical presence. It comes from the heart, and while my heart continues to beat, our love continues to be real and present. Therefore, the other advice I found impossible to implement or accept was being told you have to let go; you have to move on. What does that even mean? I did survive this, but so did our love.

Please understand, in everything I did and everything I learned, nothing took away the grief. Grief marches to its own drum, and I had to let the grief out of my body long after I felt I had come to terms with the fact that Don had died.

What makes me equipped to write this book? Well, I am, with regret, an expert on losing the most influential, precious person in my life, and I was repeatedly told during my grieving that I had a unique experience and perspective on death. I also started writing, letting the words flow, without any conscious aim to publish a book, then it became something I was being driven to do and readings confirmed this. The semi-silent co-author Don, provided material for the story and I'm sure, guided my words to some extent. It happened as it was meant to.

While in business together, Don and I had never followed traditional thinking or methodology. Every situation was viewed with innocence and solutions had to be heartfelt. Because I had little experience with death, I was an open canvas with a propensity to apply innocence and curiosity when looking for solutions to surviving unbearable pain.

I'm one of those people who needs to find the solution to a puzzle. Life had become a giant conundrum, so I started to work things through. From my perspective, there is no single answer and there is no cure, but my grieving rollercoaster had some incredibly precious moments amongst the pain. I experienced *good* grief.

This is our story, from our hearts to yours.

Part 1:
"I can't believe you left me!"

Life and death are one thread, the same line viewed from different sides.

Lao Tzu

*I*n grief, nothing makes sense. The hardest part of starting to write this book was deciding what was the beginning and what was the end. There are too many potential beginning points and there isn't really an end. So, to make sense of this, my story starts at the only logical beginning, which is also the end.

On the 4th December, 2017 at 4am, Don, my partner of thirty-seven years, died suddenly when his heart stopped. He was my world and a unique piece of humanity, and it feels too clinical to say he had a heart attack. The Australian Heart Foundation advise there is one death from a heart attack every sixty-seven minutes. I don't want him to be reduced to a statistic, so, to me, he died when his heart stopped, and there's no published statistic for that. Semantics, but it works for me.

Although we were extremely devoted to each other, we were both independent and strong, but he was still my world, as I was his. When Don died, he left a hole in so many people's lives, but me, I fell into the hole he left. I was shattered.

Part I of this book introduces the 'characters' and recounts the time that surrounded Don's death. I have a keen sense of humour and perspective that I hope makes this book easy to read; however, Part I was more difficult to write with any levity but it sets the scene for Part II, which holds the important messages from my perspective and Don's.

Before you read on, I would also like to say that *some events only made sense or took on a different significance well after Don died.*

Circumstances don't make the man, they reveal him...

Epictetus

1

The characters are real characters

May 1980 – December 2017

If our life was a movie, it would be a comedy. Throughout the story that follows, I reveal more about who we are to put a situation in context but feel it's only fair to give you a sense of us before you start a guided tour through my darkest days, and into the light, in the following pages.

I met Don in 1980 when I was eighteen. Although I had been asked out previously, I'd refused everyone. I wasn't looking for 'Mr Right'; I just wasn't looking. I was a student nurse and one of four girls. My life was small.

Then, my best friend introduced me to her 'future brother-in-law', who was in a long-distance relationship with her sister. Don was thirty-six, had been married, separated and then widowed with three children. He had lived in three countries, been a speedway rider and he'd had numerous careers. He was an entrepreneur and knew exactly who he was.

I had avoided meeting him several times, but when it did happen it was serendipitous. Neither of us were looking for a relationship, and definitely not from this meeting, but life is funny like that; it gives you exactly what you need when you didn't even know you were looking for it. Don and I went on dates, but before committing to a relationship with me, he met with his 'long-distance girlfriend' and they officially broke up. I never felt I broke their relationship, I stepped into one that had been severely cracked about two years earlier.

You may have already guessed that due to our ages that our relationship shocked a lot of people. I would also like you to pause here and gauge your reaction to our relationship at this point. This request will make sense later.

It was scandalous only because people thought their opinion on our relationship mattered. On occasion, people would ask if I was his daughter (I looked even younger without makeup). Don laughed, while I *acted* offended. But we were secure in the fact that we didn't need more than the two of us in our relationship, so people's acquiescence wasn't required. It did hurt though.

It only took a few months (well maybe six to twelve months for some) before most people accepted that our relationship was just meant to be. I didn't take on any of the judgement towards our relationship from others but must acknowledge that Don's children had the hardest adjustment to make. It wasn't easy but mostly they were great, and it worked itself out in the end.

Don had been adamant he was never getting married again, so when he proposed, I know he was as shocked as I was by what he said. It was his heart that had spoken.

We married and had two children born on the same day six years apart. The first was born nine days early and the second was born ten days late. Our eldest's biggest complaint was always that her younger brother *took* her birthday.

The characters are real characters

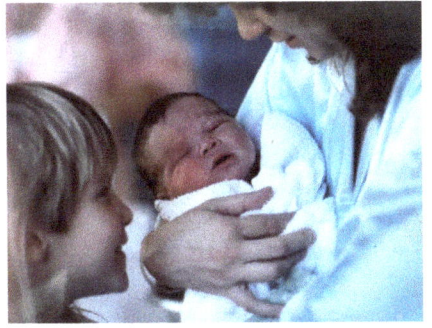 

Our two beautiful children that were born and raised out of love, are wonderful funny intelligent human beings and are part of our legacy.

Anastasia, aka Stacey, is *our* eldest and Don's fourth child. She wants to be referred to as Ashleigh in this book because she says it is the only chance she has to determine her own name (No Ashleigh's are named in the writing of this book).

Harley, *our* second and Don's fifth child arrived on his sister's birthday. After disrupting everything on the day he was born, he has been casual about life since. Mess with your sister's life – job done on day one!

Life was never normal or boring. Don and I were opposites in so many ways, but we both had a shiny moral compass, sharp intellect and keen sense of humour, which made us not only the perfect partners but also the best of friends.

We worked together for twenty-three years, and people regularly told us they would have killed their spouse had they worked with them. We were together 24/7 and loved it!

Instead of lording his maturity over me, Don encouraged me to know myself and my limitless capabilities and supported and encouraged me in everything I did, even the things I didn't think I wanted to do.

For example, I was small (5' 2" and 47kg), and Don encouraged me to drive every truck he bought, which included a Ford 40ft pantechnicon, an International with a crash gearbox and an articulated Mack truck. I could just see over the steering wheel, and, for Don, seeing the shocked looks on truck drivers' faces as they drove towards us was priceless. I was too focused on the road to notice.

Don was an entrepreneur, and I was super-organised. In business we had massive highs and frightening lows, but we were a team and we made sure we laughed, even when we thought we couldn't. We had the most hilarious conversations every day.

We had such a strong connection that I would routinely stop mid-sentence because I had said enough for Don to understand. We didn't have to explain how something affected us; we knew how the other felt and were ready with the appropriate support. We held hands everywhere we went.

Our wedding anniversary was a bigger celebration for us than anything else. It was important. But every time we were out, we would tell friends it was our anniversary. It took a while before they realised how many anniversaries we celebrated each year.

My wine glass was always the fuller one. I would switch glasses when I had less wine than Don and would even hold the glasses together to gauge levels, but although he would pretend not to notice he couldn't help smiling.

Don had children at home when we met and his youngest, Scott was at home and a wonderful big brother to Stacey when she was born. Then Harley came six years later and being a GenY boy he stayed at home for so long. When Harley moved out, Don and I were finally on our own for the first time in over thirty-five years.

Our age difference was only evident at the very beginning and at the very end. The time from our first meeting to when we were parted by death was the most incredible journey that overflowed with adventure, companionship, love and laughter.

from my heart to yours ...

Our life movie would definitely be a comedy and we would be portrayed as funny carefree characters who just took what life served and made sunshine.

Our life wasn't perfect and there were difficult times, but we made a point of having fun and enjoying what we had when we had it. The bad times simply brought us closer together and reinforced what was really important in our life. Love for each other, family and friends.

In the 37 years we had together, we only had 18 months on our own. I never imagined that would be part of our story. We had plans that would never be, but I don't regret any of our life together and am so grateful for what we did have in abundance, love and laughter.

Please don't wait until you lose someone before you truly appreciate what you have. Live the life you have everyday so there is no room for regrets.

Life is what happens to us while we are making other plans.

Allen Saunders

2

The beginning of the end

2nd December – the last couple of days before Don left this world

Life was just too busy, but we had a break coming. On Don's seventy-fourth birthday, Tuesday 5th December, we were flying to Melbourne for our first holiday in four years. We had booked the trip in October thinking December would be when things 'settled down'. I know, life is not like that; we were delusional, or, at the very least, naïve.

Don had picked Melbourne, so he was initially keen to go but then didn't talk about it or show any interest in going. 'That's okay,' I thought, '*I'm excited enough for both of us and he'll join me in this state of mind when it's time to leave.*' I chose to ignore the fact that Don kept forgetting we were going, but now I believe *he already knew, on some level, that we weren't actually going*.

On any other weekend we would get up late then go for brunch, but not this weekend. Don had organised for our son's brother-in-law, Jason, to come in early so they could get some stump grinding done. This was a semi-regular arrangement. Jason would do the heavy work like tree lopping, and Don would supervise, lend a hand or leave Jason to it while we went for brunch.

It was a hot Saturday morning. Instead of just helping, Don worked alongside Jason, who was fifty years younger than he was. It was crazy!

It was so easy to forget how old Don was, and, to this day, I do not reveal his age without showing his photo.

Family photo taken at our children's birthday 6 months before Don died. He is 73 years old and trying out a new selfie stick.

Although he appeared about ten to fifteen years younger than he was, there were some age-related ailments cropping up. His hearing wasn't 100 percent. Don's dad had suffered some hearing loss and, as a result, was often on the outside of conversations. Don would never have wanted to be the 'old man' not included in conversations. He brought fun or a depth of knowledge into every conversation and was, throughout his life, a master communicator. This was important to him; therefore, he had become diligent about protecting the hearing he had and always wore ear protection.

The beginning of the end

On this Saturday, Don gave his earmuffs to Jason to wear. I asked him why he'd done that. It was automatic for Don to put others first and I believe he forgot his hearing concerns and was just more concerned with Jason's hearing. It wasn't a conscious decision and therefore my question surprised him. He'd automatically done it because it just seemed right at the time. *I believe now that Don no longer felt the need to futureproof his hearing.*

On Sunday they started early in the garden again, and that night we were going to our daughters for dinner. This was a regular invitation, but I expected Don to say he was too tired. He didn't; he wanted to go.

At dinner, he was always the conversation manager, the umpire, the joker, and this night was no exception. He even made one of his trademark 'love life' statements about living in the best bloody country in the world! Later in the night, tiredness took over and he was quieter than usual.

Don was like a young Santa Claus, although there was no white hair or beard; he was jolly and kind and giving and huggable. We would always hug our daughter before we left. This time, she asked her dad whether she'd received her hug yet, knowing she had, but Don gave her another. Maybe she knew on some level as well that this was the last hug.

I would usually drive to a destination and Don would drive home. For most of our years together he was the self-appointed designated driver. Of course, I'm drinking my wine and half of his by switching glasses, so it was a good arrangement. This time, he asked if I minded driving home.

On the way home he asked me a random question. He asked, "Have I ever done anything that you really didn't like?"

We had a short conversation on this, and, for the record, I didn't have a list. It is the fact that he even asked the question and the timing of it that makes it part of this story.

We fell into silence as I suppose we both processed the conversation. I was confused by it. I figured in a couple of days – probably while on holiday – I would be asking him why he felt he had to ask the question. Now wasn't the time. But there wasn't going to be an opportunity and, essentially, he had just *cleared the air on any last-minute unsaid apologies he should make*.

We got home late and would have gone straight to bed but I felt we needed to order our son's Christmas present before going to bed. We were each choosing pieces that would specifically mean something to him. I knew Don was tired, but *I had a strong feeling that time was running out* and I assumed my concern was about Christmas delivery.

That done, we went to bed. We usually play a word game and read before going to sleep but Don said, "Love you, Pam." I said, "Love you, Don," and he went straight to sleep.

At 4am he jerked in his sleep and cried out. I thought he must have been having a nightmare. Not that he usually does, but there was no other explanation. I tried to wake him, and every time I pushed his shoulder, he grunted but didn't wake.

I rang our daughter and said, "I can't wake your father." She said, "It's 4am, why would you want to?" Then she told me to ring emergency. I asked her what the emergency number was. *My brain was on some sort of standby function.* There was little being processed in my mind at this time.

She said that she was on her way and would be ringing her brother as well.

The beginning of the end

I rung 000. The operator told me the first thing to do was to turn the lights on and unlock the door for the paramedics, who were on their way. The hospital was literally 'just around the corner', so although I was reluctant to leave Don, I immediately did what was asked. It wasn't going to take them long at all. Just following instructions meant I didn't need to think too much. I was numb.

The operator asked a lot of questions, including, "Do you know how to give CPR?" I said, "No," even though I did have that knowledge somewhere in my brain. I was too scared to say yes in case, in my current state, I didn't do it right and was then responsible for Don dying. Nothing was real. The operator talked me through it, and I just kept following instructions.

I had to pull Don onto the floor, which just seemed wrong. Given the weight difference there was no way I could gently lower him. He had to fall. Doing this to someone you have never intentionally hurt is really hard but, in my heart, I knew it wouldn't matter. A part of me knew he had already gone and wouldn't feel it. Ever.

The paramedics arrived and took over CPR from me. Then another team arrived, then our children. It was crowded, but everyone was there for Don.

I sat quietly on the bed, aware of what they were doing but trying desperately to think positive thoughts. One paramedic was obviously assigned to me. He was respectfully hovering.

I remember saying to our daughter, "But it's not his time yet." He had always said he would live to the ton (100 years), and I had truly believed he would. But no-one leaves by accident; they go when it's their time. I'm saying that now. I could not have admitted to it then, just in case.

This is the sort of situation that answers the question, 'Do you believe in God?' If you can call on a higher power to save a loved one's life, of course you will try. It's the ultimate 'phone a friend'. Although disillusioned with organised religions, I did believe in a higher power and angels.

I asked the angels to restart Don's heart. They didn't. This would have been a short book if they had! He would have come back only if it was meant to be. I also knew, in my heart, that although he wasn't in the body lying on the floor, he was still here.

I've heard people, probably in movies, say 'but I would know if he/she were gone'. Don and I were so close, *I* would know if he was gone. I experienced no sense that our connection was severed. I did not feel his absence on any level. I did not feel that he had ceased to exist. I never *felt* he was gone.

I thought Don had been pronounced dead four hours after he cried out in his sleep, but my daughter tells me it was forty-five minutes. This time was agonising. They had worked on him for forty-five minutes, even though he had never responded to anything they did. Thankfully, both of our children witnessed how everything that could have been done to bring him back had been done.

It was incomprehensible that he was gone. Don was always larger than life. Full of life. He was incredibly healthy 'for his age and regardless of his age'.

Being there at this time gave us irrefutable firsthand knowledge that the impossible had happened. I know if I had not been there, I would have questioned how this could be. It was confirmed on that day that Don was, in fact, mortal. Unbelievable.

By the time they stopped CPR, there were four paramedic teams on site because it was shift change. In addition, because he

The beginning of the end

died at home, we were waiting on detectives, also delayed due to shift change.

This was a blessing. *Don's body wasn't taken out of our home until six hours after he had died.*

Despite knowing he wasn't in 'the body', I could not bear to leave the physical form that remained there. This time was precious. I lay on the floor with him and only left when I was asked to answer some questions, with the Detectives, downstairs, and then I went straight back to be beside Don. I was joined by our children, and we lay on the floor with him until they took him away. I felt the warmth and saw the colour slowly draining from his body. It was surreal. At this time, I was aware opportunities to connect with Don in any way were significantly reduced and soon they would take him away and all opportunities would be gone. I suppose this is why the following photo was taken.

The one thing I could not do was watch him being carried out of our home. I didn't want that image to stay with me. I went downstairs. Our son-in-law was not asked to help carry him out either because he had lost his father three months earlier.

Taking Don's body up twenty steps to the road was going to be incredibly difficult, but Stacey and Harley were determined. Stacey says she felt honoured to be able to do this for her dad.

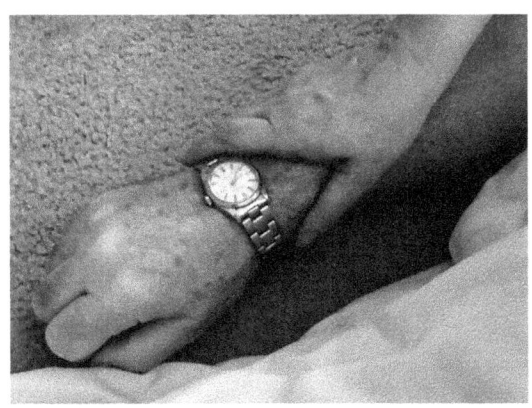

This one last photo is somehow poignant without being raw or gruesome. We always held hands and his watch was his wedding ring. Till death do us part…

Harley says it was the least he could do for the man who had carried him all *his* life. Don's son and daughter in Sydney had distance as a factor in their grieving as well. Everybody processes loss differently, so even though we all lost the same man, not one of us had the same grief to process or process for grieving.

It was the most devastating event, but I have no regrets on how it unfolded. The paramedics and police were incredibly compassionate and experienced at dealing with death. At all times, Don's body was treated with respect. I felt everything that could be done was done. Don hadn't suffered.

It sounds like I had it all together. But nope! That came much later. I was devastated. When Don left, the life was sucked out of me. I felt like a hollow shell. The outside looked the same to others and in the mirror, but inside there was nothing. A polite smile, when attempted, never reached my eyes for a long time.

I have highlighted the significant points, but the cornerstone of these happenings is that Don was preparing to go. His unexpected death wasn't avoidable. It was meant to be. At the time, I was in shock and my brain couldn't get past the fact that he had left me. But being analytical, I started examining every minute leading up to 4am on D-day, and only through hindsight could I gain an appreciation of what had really happened.

I think getting past any thinking that his death was avoidable was the first step for me. And these seemingly insignificant crumbs helped me understand:

- ♡ Don did not have a memory problem, but he kept forgetting about the holiday. I am sure this was because he knew we weren't going to Melbourne.
- ♡ He suddenly no longer felt the need to futureproof his hearing.

- ♡ He wanted to clear the air with any previously unsaid apologies he could make to me.
- ♡ He made our last shared moments perfect. He died in bed beside me with his last words being, "Love you, Pam."
- ♡ And what if I also knew on some deep level?
- ♡ I had a strong feeling that time was running out and we had to order Harley's present before going to bed. This seems materialistic but it helped because it gave him a presence at Christmas with the precious gifts he left.
- ♡ I could have questioned his changes in behaviour, but I never did. Was I telling myself, don't go there, you don't want to know?
- ♡ And why did I never 'feel' he was gone?

I have always had a positive attitude to life and looked for the silver lining in life's experiences that sucked. I had to find some light in this dark event. It was like a puzzle you can't leave. So, I looked for bits that would lighten my heavy heart.

I am thankful that his last words to me were, "Love you, Pam," and for the fact that Don died in bed beside me, and I woke when he died. This was a gift. I have no doubt Don planned it this way, knowing what it would mean to me, after. It was perfect. It was my piece of light in the dark.

Don had a habit of waking about 2am and going into the home office, returning to bed two to three hours later as he *always made sure* he was in bed beside me when I woke. I could not bear the thought of him dying in the office or alone. I never had to wonder what happened or whether my being there could have changed anything. It doesn't matter that I know nothing would have changed the time he was to die; *my mind would have deluded me into thinking I could have changed it.*

Our bedroom had always been a peaceful space for both of us. Neither of us ever sent the other one to sleep in another room – we didn't have that right. We never took a disagreement or anger into the bedroom. We made a point of clearing the air before going to bed. It was our safe haven, and for the unbearable end of our life together to happen in this room was perfect.

from my heart to yours...

Some people were horrified that Don died in our bed beside me. To them it wasn't a gift but the makings of a nightmare. Same situation, two opposing perspectives on it.

I didn't get to choose how and when Don died, but I still had to find peace with a situation I could not change. I focused on his last words to me because they are precious. I could have forgotten this in my grief, but I went looking for the pieces of light. *You cannot change a situation, only the way you choose to view it.*

I have heard of situations where people on their deathbed have taken their last breath the moment a loved one has left the room. To me, they have done this purely to save them the pain of remembering the last breath being taken.

I know of another whose husband held on for weeks in a coma and took his last breath when her friend arrived from overseas and came into the hospital room. He didn't leave her until her support had arrived. Whatever your situation, I hope you can find the love in it.

If you feel regret over a missed opportunity to see them 'one more time'. Stop! This thinking serves no purpose and distracts you from what is really important. Love isn't a short frequency. You don't have to be beside someone to love them or for them to feel your love. Love is all that matters. Treasure that connection and let go of anything that clouds it.

Regret for something that cannot be changed has no value to you or to their memory. Grief is bad enough, so choose not to carry additional baggage. If possible, look for the piece of light in whatever situation you have, and if you can't find it, wait until you are not consumed by grief and then look again.

Everyone can master a grief but he that has it.

William Shakespeare

3
But I wasn't ready...

4th December – the day Don left this world

After Don's body was taken away, I went downstairs. Our children phoned family in other states and countries as well as some local friends. My employer was also informed that I would not be on the morning teleconference. Of course, I was in no condition to discuss workload reallocation for the holiday that was due to start the next day. The much-anticipated holiday that just wasn't meant to be. It was surreal.

Family and friends arrived. Everyone was shocked. Don had always radiated life. It was unimaginable that he could be dead. *If this could happen to Don, it could happen to any one of us!*

I sat on the couch and had no words. I was incredibly calm and accepting – yeah right, I was in shock. *I know my brain put me into this state to protect me when I couldn't protect myself.* Without this haze I could not have coped.

The task of letting people know Don had died fell to our children because I couldn't and wouldn't speak to anyone. I was at a loss as to how I could put something so raw into sentences for someone else. I know this was devastating for our children, and I don't know if I offered much comfort to them at this time. I truly was dead inside. There was nothing in me to give.

What I appreciated most was that people knew how close Don and I were and how devastating this was. *I didn't have to pretend to be stronger than I was.* Mostly, they left me on the side, so I could process it in my own way. In reality, I think my daughter and son hovered and ran interference, so I didn't have to converse.

I found listening to people giving me advice on grief particularly difficult. I just nodded and gave as little back to the conversation as possible. Having timeframes put around my grief seemed cold. Having my grief compared to their experiences seemed irrelevant. I desperately wanted people to just leave me alone, but I know I was also terrified of being on my own.

Interestingly, I could recognise the people who had experienced significant loss. They were the ones who offered few words but somehow gave more comfort.

I overheard a 'friend' advising someone that he was going to just regularly pop in and that they should do the same. That got through my cloud of despair. I told my daughter I would be staying at her house and just coming back to 'keep my foot in the door', and to feed Winnie, our monster of a cat.

Before, Winnie was *our* cat. Now, Winnie's position in the hierarchy was elevated. It was just the two of us. Winnie, officially named Winston Montgomery III, is a 7.5kg Persian Russian Blue. His

Winnie uses his size to his advantage and usually ends up the only one who is comfortable.

name fit the circumstances of securing his place in the family. Don had a library of books on the world wars. He admired Winston Churchill and built a stand-up desk before they were popular because Winston Churchill was using one in 1953.

We'd already had one cat called Winston. If I needed to encourage Don to be on board with getting a kitten, I named it Winston. (How could he refuse? It was a namesake.) So, Winnie was the third Winston, and Montgomery was an army general, and his name was added in case the name Winston wasn't enough this time.

I have a 'crazy cat lady' mug. I love cats and always wanted Winnie to sit on my lap, but he would jump up on the couch next to me, then walk across me to sit on Don's lap. Winnie may have been considerate of my allergies, but I don't think so. I choose to believe that my legs were just not big enough for his mammoth frame to be comfortable.

Decision made. I was staying with our daughter and coming back to feed Winnie.

Fortunately, or unfortunately, my brain felt the need to analyse everything. What was going through my head after Don's body had been taken away? I was just sitting on the couch and thinking, *'Why can't I feel that he's gone?'* There is an expectation that when you are close, you will *feel* their lack of presence.

Before Don died, I would have said the same. *I would know* if Don wasn't there. If he ceased to exist! But I did not feel any different. I actually felt he was still with me, and close. I felt he was witnessing the distress over his death. He knew how much his death would hurt us. The following thought kept playing on my mind, *'Why can't I feel he is gone? Is it because I can't feel anything?'*

So many questions were going through my analytical brain. Being in my head was not a good place to be when I was shattered. I didn't want to engage in only internal dialogue, so when I was alone, I spoke to Don out loud. I never once thought it was falling on dead/deaf ears. I was rambling and talking out loud, which meant I couldn't easily deny or dismiss what I was saying.

I felt this spontaneous, unfiltered speech was coming from a place in my brain that was actually functioning and therefore understood what I couldn't comprehend yet. Sometimes I was baffled by what I was saying. The main one being, "I can't believe you left me." as if he had made a choice and just driven off. I was saying it in my head and out loud. I couldn't get past this. On some deep level I thought it impossible for him to have left me, although by addressing this to him I was in fact saying I know you are still here. I found life was full of contradictions.

It seemed impossible that everything was the same and different at the same time. Surely it could only be one or the other? But it was both, at the same time.

I appeared to be thinking he made a choice to leave when he did because one of the hardest parts for me to understand was why he died *before* our holiday. Why couldn't it be after we had shared that week together? So, I was also asking him, "Why couldn't we have the holiday together first so I would have that last memory of just us?"

It had been so long since we'd had a break. It was important for me/us and he blew it! He pulled out too soon! This was so incredibly unfair. I went from needing a break from chronic stress to being in the most stressful situation imaginable.

I know it was grief talking when I said some horrible, stupid things to myself and to Don. I was experiencing bits of anger. I was beside myself with grief and was trying to get him to see *he needed to come back.*

I had never experienced this amount of pain before. It was mental, emotional and physical. It was a tsunami of feeling that I could not prepare myself for or protect myself from. My mind kept taking me back forty-plus years to when my aunty was sedated after her seventeen-year-old son died in a work accident. I now knew that level of grief and wished for a break from reality. But I am not one for taking pills for anything. I couldn't even think about deadening how I felt on this. Pills just weren't going to be an option for me.

I had seen Homer Simpson experience the five stages of grief in fifteen seconds, so I was vaguely aware of the stages. But how is that even relevant? You just deal with every emotion as it comes up. It doesn't matter that someone has analysed people in their darkest moments and summarised it for us. Going through those stages is an emotional rollercoaster. Yeah, I got that, I was living it.

One of the phrases I always used on my immediate family was, "Everything happens for a reason." Bullshit! If he had to go, why couldn't we have had the holiday together first?

from my heart to yours...

Shakespeare's quote on grief at the beginning of this chapter is perfect. I wasn't managing but that was okay. Shakespeare said so.

Grief, in itself, is impossible to navigate. You live it, you don't manage it. It just is! What you manage are your actions and reactions to how you are processing grief, and you manage what you allow others to see. But sometimes you can't 'manage' anything until later.

I cannot stress enough how important the *talking out loud* was to me through the darkest time of my life. I was fighting reality because reality sucked, and it didn't seem real. So, talking out loud allowed me to sense check what I was saying to myself.

Out loud I couldn't deny what I had said and how inane, destructive or incorrect some of it was. I corrected myself more times than not. In my darkest times and in incredible pain, I was just so mean to me and Don. Don loved working and I accused him of leaving because he wasn't working at a high level anymore. I asked if he had pulled out early. I was angry at him for leaving. I told myself how stupid I was for being so emotional. I hated myself for the rawness of my emotions and my inability to control anything. I felt worthless because I couldn't function. I hated the me I saw in the mirror who reflected pain, weakness, vulnerability. Hearing what I was saying made me stop. It could too easily have spiralled out of control.

Speaking out loud is like hearing someone else say the unacceptable to you, which makes the decision easier not to accept it from yourself either.

*Believe nothing,
no matter where you read it,
or who said it,
no matter if I have said it,
unless it agrees with
your own reason
and your own common sense.*

Buddha

4
You are who you think you are

When Don died, I was in shock and my brain was avoiding processing anything. Beliefs, however, can be so deeply held that they hold onto us despite impaired mental capacity. Below I have listed the beliefs Don and I formed through our life experiences. They were not reliant on others' validation.

These beliefs were intact when I had no sense of reason left, but they were also open to expansion or adjustment. I was in new territory, and I learned a lot about life and death from the moment Don died.

Both Don and I had attended Methodist/Christian Sunday School as kids, but churchgoing hadn't stuck with either of us. We had both received the obligatory lectures on God, Heaven, Hell and judgement. Our view on each of these had shifted over time but, essentially, we lived life believing in always doing the right thing for the right reason.

These were our beliefs on the day Don died:

- ♡ We knew you can connect and communicate with passed people and spirit guides because we had both experienced this.

- ♡ We are a soul (eternal) having a human (mortal) experience.

- ♡ God/s, Source, Higher Power, Universe, Buddha, etc. are the same 'energy' that is interpreted differently by

- people, religions, cultures (referred to in this book as *Higher Power et al.*).

- Our human existence (aka life) is for learning and growth. It's not a holiday. So, don't expect every day to be sunny. Challenges are not something going wrong, they are the lessons we are here to learn from.

- Love is the only thing that survives death and is the glue in our life purpose.

- We reincarnate. Don and I knew, without knowing specifics, that we'd had many previous lives together.

- We plan our lives before we get here with challenges to overcome. If you ignore the lesson of a challenge it will repeat until you get it (I learned this one the hard way). *'Why is this always happening to me?'* Sound familiar?

- There are no accidental deaths. There is a purpose to every life and every death, although this is not always evident to us.

- Don and I do not believe in Hell, except the one some people create for themselves in this life. It is our view that the concept of Hell, a dominant premise in religions, is used to control through fear and judgement.

- We didn't have a clear view on Heaven except we know there is a place we go to between lives. But if we believed religions were misleading about Hell, what do we believe about their place called Heaven?

- Judgement (after life). Nope, we're not buying it. *Higher Power et al.* is love – that's it. Judgement is ego-based. Ego is a trait of human beings. Spirituality is absence of ego.

So, our beliefs placed Don somewhere good; there was no fear or guilt to deal with, and I knew I would be able to contact him. But I was now living in Hell on Earth. *My* life was an issue because I didn't want it. The future was too bleak and painful to comprehend. What life could I have when the love that defined my life was gone?

As the shock wore off, the questions started and were highlighting gaps in our understandings that I hadn't been aware of until I needed to understand WTF had just happened! Such as:

- ♡ Did the Don I know cease to exist, and was his soul different from 'my' Don?

- ♡ How much does he see, hear, feel (emotionally) where *he is?*

- ♡ How much does he see, hear, feel (emotionally) where *I am?*

- ♡ Does he feel my pain? I knew he was the only person who would fully appreciate my level of suffering, but only if he was still 'my' Don. We shared everything, so were we sharing this tragic event?

- ♡ When can I connect with Don? I was desperate for this one to be answered.

from my heart to yours...

I understand people's beliefs are acquired through their culture, upbringing and religious affiliation and life experiences. I am not here to judge anyone's life or choices because we all have the freedom of choice and are on our own journey.

The main belief I had acquired that helped me was the understanding that only Don's body had died. Feeling that Don was still here, and that I could reconnect with him, was my lifeline and became my focus.

I was so grateful for this understanding because it enabled me to find him and then for *him* to help me through this horrific event, *like no-one else could* because he gave me an empowering perspective on life that I could only appreciate through his death.

If you live to be a hundred, I want to live to be a hundred minus one day, so I never have to live without you.

Winnie the Pooh
A. A. Milne

5
"When you die..."

Over the years, Don and I had light-hearted conversations about who would go first.

The first time this was discussed would have been in our first few years together, and the last time being a few months before Don died (that's a conversation over approximately thirty-five years). The reluctance to be left without the other was paramount for both of us. So, we settled on going together – it wasn't a pact; it was a way of ending the light-hearted conversation of a seemingly impossible conundrum.

In a more recent light-hearted conversation, Don was asked, "Could Pam have a new partner after you go?"

He said, "I'll haunt her if she does."

I said, "Right answer, you don't get to leave me just because you're dead!"

Don was not sick; it was just one of those random conversations. We had an uncanny closeness. From the first time we met we felt a deep connection and were unbelievably comfortable with each other. Our relationship had ups and downs, especially at the start when the age difference wasn't necessarily easy for us or acceptable to others. But we had an unbreakable bond that held us close through everything.

Don knew, with half a sentence, what I was talking about. We regularly found we were thinking random things at the same time – words weren't always necessary – and we instinctively knew how the other felt. We could not have been closer.

Therefore, when Don died, I couldn't believe he had ceased to exist, but his side of the bed was undeniably empty. The dishes also weren't getting done. As much as I wanted to believe that he would come back when he saw how devastating his leaving was for me, I sort of understood there was no Ctrl Z (undo).

I continued to speak to him out loud when no-one could hear; it was just the two of us. I told him he was the only one who could understand the loss I was suffering, so, of course, he was the one I had to discuss my loss with.

In life, Don and I had a strong belief that our love and connection was so solid that we could not be separated. Later, we discovered we'd had previous lives together. Although we didn't know anything specific about this, it just made sense. It also explained our first meeting when there was an immediate feeling of recognition that was quickly shoved aside by reality saying, *'Not possible, you've only just met.'* Later, we understood the zap of awareness was our souls saying, *'There you are, I've been looking for you.'* **Love is eternal.**

from my heart to yours...

"You don't get to leave me just because you're dead." That's one of those light-hearted statements you make but know there is a deeper meaning in it. I was making a joke and being deadly serious in this statement.

I think the hardest part with death is the intense shock that all opportunities have ceased. No more hugs, no discussions, no coffee, no sharing. For me, like so many others, it wasn't a wind down, it just was there one day and not the next. You feel there

"When you die..."

are things you still want to say, there are new questions you want answered. You want there to be a reason they need to come back. It doesn't matter how much you have said, 'I love you' in the past, the one time you can't say it to them because they've gone, is the most important one. You go into shock.

But love doesn't die. I still felt strongly connected to Don, and this belief alone paved the way for what was to come next for me. I knew in my heart it was only a matter of time before we reconnected. I was desperate to connect and strongly believed that Don would also be wanting to make contact with me. Wherever he was. This was a lifeline. Love doesn't die.

I felt that with this belief I had not lost all opportunities. I had hope. You can survive anything if you can just hold onto even a slither of hope.

Know that you have choices here – what you choose to believe in and what you choose to do.

Part II:
Looking for Don

When it hurts to look back and you're afraid to look forward, just look beside you, I will be there.

Unknown

The loneliness started the moment Don's body left our home. This quote became a mantra because I needed to believe he was beside me. It aligned with my belief that Don's body had died but that his soul was still connected to me.

I told Don what my mind was thinking, and I sounded rational, but at the same time I was in the most unbearable pain, and it was unrelenting.

My brain was constantly trying to work everything out, make sense of it. My whole life I have been a problem solver. I couldn't just accept that there was nothing I could do to make this better in some way, any way.

The first thing I had to do was make contact with Don, and it never occurred to me that it wouldn't be possible. This also gave me something I wouldn't have thought was possible at this time: I had something in my future I could look forward to.

I must point out here that my mind and my heart were on two separate journeys. I was a fractured person. My heart ached and nothing provided relief. My emotions were out of control; grief built to the point where my body had to release it, and it did, and it was completely involuntary. My mind, however, was also busy trying to come up with something that would help reduce my suffering. It rationalised everything, and it tried to be understanding but was impatient with my emotional side. I was at war with myself and life.

My mind desperately needed to find him and connect with him *and I knew in my heart that Don was still with me*, but where? I needed to find him...

*I believe in
the immeasurable power
of love; that true love
can endure any circumstance
and reach across any distance.*

Steve Maraboli

6

Not just my partner but a part of me

6th December – two days after Don left this world

Two days after Don died, I went to see Andy. He's not a reader, but an energy healer whom Don and I had been seeing for Reiki sessions periodically for a few years. During sessions, Andy would also pass on messages received from spirits that were significant for the healing of the stuck energy.

Seeing Andy was something I felt driven to do without fully questioning or understanding why. Mostly, I was on autopilot. I knew without a doubt that I had to go specifically to Andy, and *my heart and mind knew I would hear from Don.*

Being an energy healer, Andy would help lift some of the grief trapped in my body. My stomach felt like it had a hard ball in it. The muscles were tight and not in a good six-pack kind of way. I was in agony.

My belief that people continue to watch over us and care about us after they are gone was a lifeline that I had a firm grip on. I was desperate to hear from Don.

Melanie, a dear friend and psychic, had introduced us to Andy about three years earlier. Before Don's death, it was me who went for sessions to resolve my health issues around chronic work stress, while Don had a cuppa and a chat with Pat, Andy's wife.

In a previous session with Andy, he had told me about communicating with his own father after he had passed some decades earlier. His father had been in, what Andy calls, the 'boarding house' for six months after he died, and Andy regularly communicated with him there.

I'd never had a reading where I had conversed with someone who had passed, but knew a few people who'd had this experience in their readings. Don's mum had come into a reading with him years earlier, but, I think, not in a convincing way.

I was learning as I was going, and ignorance helped me as I didn't realise people are not immediately able to communicate after they die. I was advised that *after crossing over, they go into a healing place/state to cleanse the spirit of the unhealthy baggage brought through from this life. It is my understanding that the healing time is dependent on how much baggage, in the form of negative emotions, you carry at the time of death and the age of your soul. The older the soul, the more experienced they are at healing 'from life'.*

Therefore, I was unlikely to get a message from Don after only two days. Andy advised me of all of this prior to starting, undoubtedly, to prepare me for disappointment.

I wasn't to be disappointed though because the moment the session started, Andy had a message from Don for me. Jeez, I love this guy! Don never failed to impress me in life, and two days in and he was exceeding our expectations in death.

Don desperately wanted me to understand that he left because, 'He didn't want to be a burden to me.' Those where the exact words he wanted passed on to me.

Andy received a vision of Don in a hospital bed, which was the alternative had he not died immediately from the heart attack. In a way, it now made sense why Don worked so hard the days before he died. Don never wanted to be sick or weak or incapacitated in any way; it was a real fear for him. If his body was starting to fail, he would be ready to go.

At Don's age, he had seen a lot of people suffer. He was a capable and proud man and could not bear the thought of being in the situations he saw so many family and friends in. He was empathetic to their situations but feared it for himself. He helped everyone but never wanted to be the one who needed help.

I knew it was something he felt strongly about, but I didn't realise the *significance this fear would have on his exit plan*. At this point, I didn't know we make exit plans, but knowing Don it made sense that he was showing an alternative life (in a hospital bed) he was not prepared to have for himself or for me. And he knew I wouldn't have wanted that for him either and would understand. He didn't want to be a burden to me, which is not how I would have looked at it, but this was his life, his decision.

Andy also passed on that Don was now in a good place. "He no longer experiences fear or pain." This wasn't said as a generalisation, it was part of Don's message verbatim. I can imagine the relief he felt in having these two elements of life now non-existent where he was. He wanted me to understand this because of the depth of our love for each other; he knew I never wanted him to suffer in any way either. *I felt some peace with this message*.

He had left on his terms; he would no longer fear losing his dignity through ill health and the ageing process, and I think it was also an indication that the arthritic type of pain in his fingers, knees and feet were worse than he let on.

Don was seventy-three when he died, the day before his seventy-fourth birthday, but he looked and acted much younger.

He must have known time was running out with his body and he didn't want to be seen or treated like an old man. I loved Don intensely, and still do. As much as I could never imagine a life for me without him in it, I never wanted him to suffer in life.

One of our beliefs was that we each come into this life with a plan (a blueprint of sorts). In all likelihood, this could also be why I knew to go to Andy. Our souls had written this into our blueprints for our first contact, and my intuition told me to follow the plan I wasn't consciously aware of, or it could be that Don whispered it in my ear.

Don't blueprint obviously did not involve ill health. He was rarely sick in his life so the likelihood he had written diminishing health from old age into his blueprint is highly unlikely. Don had, however, started experiencing some age-related ailments that he was managing but refused to be defined by.

'I did it my way' was one of Don's funeral songs. You won, Don. You did it your way! And he did, in life and right up until he took his last breath. I loved him for his strength of character and realising that even his exit was according to his terms warmed my heart. But knowing this did not stop the grief and pain and tears. I found nothing alleviated that, but when I focused my thoughts only on Don, I was so extremely happy *for him* and could feel a fragment of peace.

So, two days after Don died, I had my first couple of messages from him:

- ♡ He didn't want to be a burden to me.
- ♡ Had he not died he would have been a version of himself he did not want to be.
- ♡ He was now in a good place, free of fear and pain.

It was exactly the sort of message he would want me to know as soon as possible. The fact he sent a message before he was 'supposed' to be able to communicate was very Don. This was how he had lived, going outside the norm, pushing the envelope, doing it his way. Anything people said couldn't be done, he proved them wrong. In this short message, I got a sense that this was *my* Don. He was just as desperate to get a message to me as I was to receive one.

So, I was starting to get an understanding of life after death, but naturally questions were forming more quickly than answers being received.

At this stage I didn't really know what Don was like; I didn't know how much of the personality survived or for how long, but this message helped reaffirm for me our continued connection through deep love.

I wondered if he would come out of the healing stage as his soul and not the personality that was the flawed, imperfect, wonderful human I knew.

But I knew where Don was and that he was within reach. This was the main detail I needed to know. This gave me an anchor. Whenever I thought about Don, where he was and that everything was perfect for him now, I felt peace. I tried as much as possible to come back to this space in my head/heart. I was experiencing constant and excruciating pain in my grief but feeling in my heart that Don was safe and well created a small safe haven.

When I thought of me, however, I was bereft. I could see no point in being here anymore. It's not that I wanted to die, I just didn't want to live. Any thoughts of the future held so much agony, and I didn't know how I could survive the pain. The day before Don died, I was strong, independent and extremely capable. After, that Pam no longer existed in my world. She had died with Don. This wasn't weakness; it is a reality that significant loss changes you, and you can never go back to who you were because you are irrevocably changed.

It's funny that even for the ones we love the most, we want them to live well into old age and feel more rightness in a death following some form of suffering. When people go earlier than this, *we* feel we have been cheated when, in fact, the loved one has 'gone on their terms'. It's a tug-o-war between the pain of seeing them suffer and the pain of them being gone.

The physical relief received from the healing was secondary to hearing from Don, but when I left the session, I wasn't choking on grief and my stomach wasn't taking my attention. Whatever grief Andy released I refilled within a few days, but there was noticeable relief for my body and mind. Don wasn't someone I was going to get over any time soon and this was only two days after he had died.

Don was not just my partner but a part of me. I came to understand the loss of the most precious person in my life was not one loss but three. Three losses to contend with all at once, so no wonder it was unbearable:

- ♡ I lost Don – no more banging around in the kitchen, no more offering (and receiving) countless hugs, no more hilarious random conversations about life nor sharing every experience.

- ♡ I lost 'Us' aka Don and Pam, and I believe the best words to define 'Us' are in Maya Angelou's quote: *"I've learned that people will forget what you said, people will forget what you did, but people will never forget how you made them feel."* 'Us' is how he made me feel: safe, loved, supported, cherished, part of an unbreakable team and 'right' in this world.

 And I lost the Pam I knew. The hardest loss to come to terms with was losing myself, after all, it was supposedly all I had left. I was changed forever and wasted so much time trying to get back to the past Pam when all I had to work with was a new Pam.

With this understanding I now also had the realisation that each of these losses provided different challenges, would heal differently and in different timeframes. No wonder grief is intense and confusing. We view death as something to avoid at all costs and this costs us in life.

from my heart to yours...

We are complex human beings, and, through grief, we go through unimaginable pain. To me, the main benefit of the various healing procedures (in this case Reiki) was to alleviate the physical manifestations of the grief in my body. No-one can take away the grief, but ask yourself, "What is happening to me that someone can ease for me?"

When you lose someone, there is a massive amount of healing ahead. When it feels overwhelming, engaging others to help you get some balance back in your body is just sensible. I recommend Reiki, massage, reflexology and kinesiology only because I have experience with those. Investigate what feels right for you.

Ask yourself, "Where is the grief manifesting in my body and what do I need?"

The most wasted day of all is that on which we have not laughed

Nicolas Chamfort

7

Second message was classic Don – he's back!

8th & 9th December – four days after Don left this world

Our life was filled with laughter, and we did in fact laugh every day, even during periods of hardship and challenges. We made sure we did. The ability to always laugh and have fun was very much a part of who we saw ourselves to be, no matter the circumstances. I lost that in a heartbeat.

I was sleeping at our daughter's house and wasn't spending much time at home because I didn't want to deal with unannounced visitors; however, I needed to be home enough that it felt like I hadn't 'left'. I couldn't bear the thought of not wanting to return to our home. So, I went home on my own, to feed Winnie every morning and afternoon and pottered around so I could feel 'at home' at home. I was exercising a careful balance between having company and having alone time.

Although we'd only been in the house for ten years, we had many wonderful memories in it and life was always fun, especially in ways that were unique to us and our attitude to life. I always attributed the reason we both looked younger than our years to our ability to laugh daily and enjoy life.

Don was undoubtedly the love of my life, but I wasn't the only one who lost him. Family and friends lost a person who was treasured, and the world lost one of life's characters. Don had the knack of finding fun in the mundane and most unlikely places. He infected people with his passion for revealing the fun in life's boring bits and kept family and friends amused via updates on Facebook.

One of his regular posts was set in our downstairs toilet with the resident elephant, Looey. The small shelf above the toilet held a plastic plant, pottery vase and wooden scrabble pieces spelling 'LOO' (just in case you wondered where you were). Don added a small elephant and named him Looey.

Before long, Looey began to take on a personality of his own as he was repositioned every time one of us used that toilet. 'Looey' moved toilet rolls to the shelf, climbed the plastic plant, abseiled down toilet paper hanging from the shelf, etc. My best attempt to 'out-do' Don's staged scenes was when I hid Looey behind toilet rolls on the shelf and, when Don found him, Looey was holding a 'picket' saying 'Boo!'

Some of Don's FB posts

Don's Looey FaceBook posts started less than one month before he left this world. He had fun and loaded quite a few

Turns out Looey has a mind of his own. Refuses to sit still in an atmosphere where most others do!

"Gaaawd, but that Looey is cunning. He has been studying the pyramid builders from ancient Egypt!"

Second message was classic Don – he's back!

What an incredible playground for a bored heffalump!   *Oooops! Get a grip on it Looey!*

posts in that time causing a friend to comment "You seem to spend a lot of time in 'that' room Don. To which Don replied, "Age, Gavin. Age is a wonderful thing!"

On one occasion, Don came out of the toilet with a big grin on his face. I used my firm voice and said, "What have you done?" Of course, the question was related to our game but a friend who was there at the time said, "Jeez, if you have to report what you do in there, I'm not using that toilet."

Four days after Don died, I was home alone feeding Winnie. While using 'Looey's' toilet, the light went off, on, off and on as if someone were turning it off and on slowly. It's an internal room so it's pitch-black with the lights off, and the light switch is located outside the room.

I freaked out. I was alone in the house. Although my first thought was that someone was in the house, I immediately knew that wasn't the case. There was no-one else there. Another logical explanation would have been a faulty lightbulb, but it wasn't flickering as if the bulb was failing. It was deliberate and slow. I can also confirm that this bulb wasn't changed for another eleven months after this; it wasn't faulty.

Of course, you may be thinking there was another explanation for such a story, so I also need to address and rule out questions on my sanity and vulnerability. Please understand that I am an intelligent person, I am methodical and analytical. I am not weak-minded or in any way suggestible. I do not accept others' views; I make up my own mind on everything.

It was Don, and I knew this somehow even though it seemed crazy. As unbelievable as it seemed, Don was communicating directly with me!

I screamed out, "If this is you, Don, please stop. It's freaking me out." The light stayed on.

I had received my first message through Andy before it was reasonable to expect any communication and now this. I really hadn't expected this; because I hadn't known he would be able to do the 'stuff' you see in movies. My expectation on any communication between us was that we would connect through a medium or clairvoyant. But this was direct communication from Don letting me know he was here, in the house, with me. My biggest problem was that I was also alone. No-one was going to believe this! I experienced it and found it hard to believe.

I always felt he was with me, that he wouldn't leave me, but can you imagine what it would be like to suddenly get a message from beyond the grave? It was unbelievable, and it was real. It was personal and precious and one of the memories I still carry close to my heart.

Every minute of every day, I was in excruciating physical and emotional pain. It had only been four days and I was facing a lifetime of pain. Photos reminded me of shared experiences that would forever be all I had, a past tense. No new experiences, no future. The future did not bear thinking about.

Do you know what the situation with the toilet light really gave me? A present-day experience that would be *added* to

Second message was classic Don – he's back!

my memories. It was a precious, priceless memory because it happened when I thought there would be no more shared experiences. Unbelievable.

My experiences with Don had shifted to another level. One that I had no idea what to expect, and my mind didn't even want to go there. All I knew was that death had not ended our relationship, it had merely changed it.

Nothing else happened after the lights flickered but it was enough. I had a lot to process, and it gave my mind something else to think about, and I even managed a slight curve of the lips when I thought about it. For someone who had laughed every day this was significant. My first semi-smile, and it was, as usual, Don who made me do it when I didn't think I could.

Naturally, I was overjoyed by the lights but had to process it mentally before sharing what had happened. How receptive would people be when they hadn't witnessed something like this themselves? I did, however, tell our daughter that night as I knew she would believe me. She was delighted. She wanted him to flick the lights for her (eye roll).

I didn't tell anyone else at this time because this mind-blowing event felt incredibly personal. I also wasn't prepared to have to convince someone else of it being real. It happened and whether people believed it or not was irrelevant.

I knew that if there was any way Don could communicate with me, he would. I had now received two messages, in two different ways.

Before Don died, I had already thought up a Christmas scene for Looey, so the next day while at our house with our daughter, I set it up. Two toilet rolls stacked with a small string of tinsel wrapped round like a tree and the end of it looped through Looey's trunk.

I set it up and turned to Stacey and said, "What do you think?" Immediately, the lights started flickering. Not like the previous off-on-off-on but like an enthusiastic flashing of approval. The timing was perfect. The lights started flickering exactly when I asked, "What do you think?"

This was Stacey's first experience of Don affecting the lights, and my second, but it was still surreal. This was far better than a medium saying, "He's here." when you can't see anything. This was Don saying, *'I'm here!'* What a guy!

I know love doesn't die. I know for me it didn't because I was expressing my love through grief, but this was Don showing *he* was still connected to me by our love. A love that transcended 'death'.

My heart was holding onto those precious messages and my analytical brain started asking more questions. I wanted to know more about this version of Don. The messages demonstrated his need to communicate; that was part of who he had been. Was I the only one suffering, or did he still love me, miss me and feel pain from our separation?

I had always held that he was the only one who would understand the magnitude of what I was feeling, but now I really wanted to know if he was suffering from our separation as well. Did he understand?

Don and I were both desperate to connect, and I was open to any form it could take. This meant I had received some grief relief within two days. I have since wondered if we had learned Morse code before Don died... But it is what it is.

I had spent a lifetime talking with this man, and now I had a couple of sentences sent to a third party and lights flickering. It was like crawling through the desert and only getting a capful of water to drink. It wasn't enough, but I would take whatever I could get.

from my heart to yours...

The saddest part of this for me is that there are undoubtedly passed loved ones sending messages that are tragically not received because people's minds are closed.

Say, "I'm ready for a message." and if you think you received a message but are not sure, know that you did receive it. Your intuition saw it and your Earth brain said, I need more proof. Listen to your heart.

Please be open to receiving, and don't worry about what others say. This is your relationship, and you are still bound to this person by love. I feel Don communicated a lot earlier than is usual so don't use my experience as a yardstick on time. Be patient.

I also send messages to Don like my final challenge for Looey

> Tears are 1% Water and 99% feelings.
>
> Unknown

8

Can crying cause dehydration?

The two weeks after Don left this world

For the first two weeks after Don died, there were a lot of days where I felt all I did was breathe and cry.

Crying over Don was inevitable. I never fought it, but I did prefer to cry alone and would escape people's company specifically because I knew the dam was going to burst.

Every time I hopped in our car to go home, alone, it would trigger an immediate outpouring of grief. It was just sitting under the surface waiting for the first opportunity to escape. I had minimal control over it and had to just let it flow until it was done.

The car was also an emotional trigger because previously I would have been driving somewhere with Don or driving home to Don. Some of my fondest memories are of the many road trips we did together. The car I was driving was one we had shared, and it was where my deepest feelings of loneliness were inescapable.

When I got home the grief would erupt out of my body, again. It would start in my stomach and push its way up. It felt bigger than the space it was in. It took my breath, and I could barely breathe while it was in motion. Then it would push through my chest and the tears would stream down my face. The volume of tears was amazing.

I decided early on that it was pointless wiping the tears as they fell, so I didn't. I figured, if I tried to wipe them away while they were in freefall, I couldn't deny that I had no control. Also, had I wiped them away, I would have had a reddened face and eyes and that would have been harder to hide from others. The only reason I wanted to hide my crying was because I didn't want discussion, sympathy or judgement. This was so deeply personal. My grief was between Don and me.

My 'go to' place to cry at home was on Don's side of the bed. I would lay on his pillow and sob until I had released everything at that time and a sense of calm would wash over me. I felt the calmness also came from Don. I have absolutely no doubt he was beside me every minute of every day and was, depending on his capabilities, either watching over me or helping me.

In addition, my pillow wore one of Don's t-shirts (for over two years and counting). I slept with my face on his shirt because it was a great comfort to me. Don had been a hugger so whenever I was sad, down or upset, I always walked into a hug. I would draw comfort from having my cheek over his heart, hearing it *ka-thump, ka-thump*. The only part of this comfort I could retain was having my cheek on his shirt on the pillow. Anything that gave me even a slither of comfort was okay with me.

Because of some of my life experiences, in particular work stress, I already knew how stress can manifest in the body. I was aware of the health issues that could eventuate by not releasing the emotions that were constantly bubbling up. I cried buckets and that was not only okay, but incredibly healthy.

I remember little about the first couple of weeks. Looking back, I was in shock from the time I couldn't wake him up. This was only obvious later, but I had no idea at the time. I felt numb to everything, which I had mistakenly interpreted as being calm, realistic and accepting.

I didn't realise my mind had put me into shock and was then gradually releasing me from the state of shock I had been suspended in. I had been told repeatedly that 'things would get better' so imagine my dismay when they actually started getting worse and worse, now that the numbness was wearing off and a new reality of my loss was kicking in.

I needed to accept I had no control over the grief monster and just let it flow, because it was too hard to act 'normal' for other people's benefit. Trying to hold grief in just allowed it to build up and then the inevitable release was more intense and painful.

I didn't realise that under stress your breath is shallower. This reduces your 'life force energy' when you really need it, as well as reducing the amount of oxygen to the brain, which is essential for mental health.

It physically hurt to take a deep breath, so I was advised by a health professional to deep breathe for fifteen minutes every morning and to take ten deep breaths every time I thought about it. I put a post-it-note on my monitor saying 'breathe'. The fifteen minutes I found incredibly difficult, it hurt too much, but I always started with *one* and did as many as I could after that.

from my heart to yours...

Initially, grief consumes you entirely and all you can do is breathe and cry.

Taking deep, slow breaths is incredibly beneficial. I know it sounds silly, but it helps to put notes around to remind yourself to deep breathe.

I also want to say that you cannot cry 'too much', and you cannot cry if the emotion isn't there for release. It is *detrimental to your health to push the emotions down and not cry*. Anyone making you feel bad about 'still' crying is doing this because your crying makes *them* feel bad. Don't listen to them; when you need to cry just do it.

*Life should not
be a journey to the grave
with the intention of arriving safely
in a pretty and well-preserved body,
but rather to skid in broadside in a
cloud of smoke, thoroughly used up,
totally worn out, and proclaiming
Wow! What a ride!*

Hunter S. Thompson

9
How I survived the funeral
12th December – eight days after Don left this world

Because I was able to spend so much time with Don's body at home after he died, I hadn't expected to want to see his body at a place like a funeral home. But given the option, I discovered I needed to be where his body was as much as possible.

Don's funeral was eight days after he died, and people arrived from other countries and states so there was a lot of activity, decisions to make and a eulogy to write. It helped to have something to do and plan. I didn't want to think about how close Christmas was.

In New Zealand, where we had both grown up and worked for many years, we had family and friends who would not be able to make it to Australia for the funeral. Therefore, a memorial service was planned for the same time with the intention of live-streaming the service. The live-stream hook-up was successfully tested days before but, on the day, the internet gods did not get the memo, and the live-streaming didn't work. As a result, his New Zealand service was officiated by our brother-in-law, with family and friends sharing their stories about Don. Essentially, Don had two separate services at the same time in two countries. Bless him.

Don's Australian funeral was not officiated by a minister. Our wedding had been 'on-stage' at Don's theatre restaurant and was officiated by his brother-in-law, a Marriage Celebrant. It was therefore fitting that Don had an Master of Ceremony

(MC) for his exit. Very Don! The MC was a dear, long-time friend, comedian and entertainer. He told us to treat the funeral as a celebration of Don's life, and, as a result, all the decisions became so much easier.

The song choices were easy. Frank Sinatra's 'I did it my way' was perfect for Don and was the opening song. The photo slideshow of an incredible life played to Louis Armstrong's 'What a wonderful world', which was also a favourite of Don's and epitomised his outlook on life. He was carried out to the same music he had chosen for both his parents' funerals: 'I will follow him' by Whoopie Goldberg in *Sister Act*.

This advice also made writing my eulogy enjoyable. I *wanted* to tell people what an incredible guy he was and how he meant the world to me. Talking about him took him out of past tense and brought him into the present. I have included the eulogy in this chapter.

I was managing at this stage but had anxiety over attending the funeral. I expected it would be more traumatic (and publicly so) than the day he had died. My fear was that it would be unbearable, and I would be uncontrollably emotional. But I wasn't. It was a celebration, and I survived.

Because I had already received messages from Don, I knew he was there, with me. I knew he could and would communicate with me. This meant that the funeral, in my mind, was a farewell of his body. I wasn't saying goodbye to him, this wasn't the end, it was a ceremony for a body he no longer needed.

We had never really discussed what he wanted to happen after he died, but we had both decided we wanted to be cremated. Ironically, although I knew I could communicate with him, it never occurred to me to ask him what he wanted. I just thought, '*I have time, I'll work out what to do with his ashes later.*'

Don said that if he could achieve the quote at the start of this chapter, he would be happy. I have no doubt he achieved this and was very happy with his life when he died. He'd ridden speedway in his youth so sliding in sideways and viewing life as a 'ride' resonated. For many, many years he told me speedway was the highlight of his life, he had loved it like nothing else. The fumes, the noise, the crowds cheering, riding a bike with no brakes, the thrill and the risk of it all. How could I compete with this? (eyeroll)

Maybe to ease his conscience, he would always follow up with, "I wish you could have seen me ride."

Ironically, I think I probably could have. I had gone to the speedway with my family when I was young, but still I wouldn't have seen him. I could never watch; I kept my head down and eyes shut whenever the bikes were racing. I wonder whether I

I'm not sure when this photo was taken but huba huba.

At a speedway meet in 1973. Don is in the black leathers 2nd from the left in both photos.

couldn't watch because he was one of the riders. I believe Don's mum watched the bike races the same way I did, with eyes tightly shut.

When Don started telling me that I was more important to him than speedway had been, that was special. He was sincere and I think a little surprised. Speedway being his life had been his mantra for so long.

He always wished I could have seen him ride, and I still think I can honour this wish. It is said that everyone's lives are stored in the Hall of Records. The Akashic Records are a vibrational recording of your entire life. I can watch, *as Don*, and experience all the emotions he felt, when I get to where he is. I promise him I will do this.

from my heart to Don's . . .

My eulogy

Don will forever be the love of my life.

He has been a pivotal part of my life for most of my life. We met when he was thirty-six and I was eighteen. The most unlikely pairing, but we knew very quickly we had a connection that was unique and would be lasting.

We were opposites in so many ways. Near the start he told me 'Don't try and change me'. I said 'Good – works both ways'. We understood in life, mistakes were inevitable and okay, and as a partner our role was to support not criticise the other. We were a team and held the deepest respect for each other as individuals.

Don showed me what courage looked like, to know myself and then stand by my convictions, to never be afraid to be different or have another opinion, to enjoy life even when times were challenging, when others say it can't be done, you prove them wrong, when you have a problem, just fix it, say what you mean and mean what you say, own what you do whether it's good or bad.

Through Don I learned life lessons that have made me the person I am today. The most important is that I know who I am. I am strong. The greatest gift he gave me is my sense of self.

The qualities Don saw in others... he had in abundance but was quick to recognise and admire these qualities in his children (5 children across 2 marriages). He was so proud of every one of them.

Don was an incredibly caring person and he admired greatly his eldest daughter's commitment to helping those that needed it most.

Don never followed the well-trodden path. He exceeded expectations himself and was so proud of his second daughter's strength, courage and determination to be the best she could be and to defy the odds.

Don purchased a computer in the early 80s that required 4 people to shift the hard drive. Very little training was available, but he worked it out. His eldest son shares Don's passion for being at the forefront of technology with a strong work ethic and a passion for learning.

Don was a great communicator but acknowledges our daughter has usurped him on this one. Her ability to talk is legendary. Together, they had their own language (some may say the filter was defective, others may say they just didn't have one) that either had us laughing or crying.

Don had a big heart and when he saw anywhere he could help another, he did. His youngest son does the same but maybe doesn't always recognise the significance of what he has done for others, yet.

Don was a very unique person. The world has lost a great man. He had a way of bringing fun into every situation and sharing so that others could enjoy the joke. His Facebook posts on hole digging, lawn mowing, and Looey are examples of this. Don saw having fun as a big part of having a happy and healthy life.

Don lives on in the hearts of the people he has met. He was a lovely genuine person who loved others and was loved in return. People responded to him. It was inevitable that a conversation with Don would include an exchange of smiles and, more often than not, chuckles.

He changed so many lives and has left this world a far better place.

Don loved life. He loved me. We were married for thirty-five years and I loved him so deeply for so long that I did not think I could bear the pain and grief of life without him. I would not trade the pain of losing him for a life less loved.

I am fortunate to have had him to share a significant part of my life with. He has a very solid place in my heart that will continue as long as my heart beats.

Don left this body last Monday. He was done with it. I'm sure he believed his body could no longer keep him in the manner to which he had become accustomed.

He helped everyone that needed help but rarely asked for help. He gave willingly but never asked for anything (except Nathan's lawnmower). He was very proud and leaves this world as he would have wanted, still strong and vibrant.

Goodbyes are only for those who love with their eyes. Because for those who love with heart and soul there is no such thing as separation.

Rumi

10

The end of the worst year ever!

The rest of the first month after Don left this world

With the funeral over and most people gone, I was still only spending short periods of time at home, but I did feel fine when I was there. A family friend suggested cleaning the energy in the house of any pain that may have been left when Don died. I was totally open to anything that could relieve my suffering, as long as Don's energy wasn't removed from the house. I felt his presence and of course he was flicking the lights every day, mainly in the kitchen and our ensuite. He was also now sending messages through music, in particular 'Perfect' by Ed Sheeran and Beyoncé. I was like Pavlov's dogs on this song. I could do nothing when it played except stand by his picture and cry. This song was us and resonated with an intensity. At this time I also received 'You are the reason' (Callum Scott) and 'Everything I do, I do it for you' (Bryan Adams), so I didn't want anything to interfere with that energy.

Melanie, our psychic medium and dear friend, offered to check for bad energy and clear it if needed. She came to do this a few days after the funeral.

She walked through the house and said there was good energy in the house, a lot of love. Yep!

She went into the bedroom and, without any input from me, actually stood where Don's body had lain on the floor for six hours. Don was there and she said she felt his presence strongly. Don immediately had a message for her to deliver.

Melanie said to me, "Don is holding you by the shoulders and looking into your eyes with that intense serious look that he has, and he is saying to you, 'You are strong, Pam, but you don't have to be strong on your own anymore. I will be strong for you.'"

The posture, intense look and words were pure Don. I had no idea what he could do in his spirit state, but Don was a sincere person. I believed him and I trusted Melanie. He also told me to sign the papers, but I didn't know what that meant. I would, however, learn more about his ability to be strong for me in a March reading.

When I felt alone, I could visualise Don holding my shoulders and promising to be my strength. It was invaluable to receive the visual cues from Melanie and not just the words.

Melanie had come into our life by accident. A couple of years earlier, during a stressful period at work, I walked past a café where Melanie was reading. I needed something to ease my stress, so I sat down for a reading. It was a Saturday and I wanted direction on how I would handle a situation when I returned to work on the Monday.

Without me saying anything, the first words from her were, "Two people at work have discredited you and it is very unfair." She had nailed it exactly. Actually, I had been so focused on one of the people (my boss) that I had pushed the other situation to the back of my mind. But yes, two people had caused me grief, and I had informed my boss that on Monday I would let her know whether I was resigning.

I have no doubt that all the people we meet come into our life for a reason. Melanie became a dear friend to Don and me and was a great help after Don died. She had a personal connection with him as well as an understanding of where he was and the ability to speak to him. When she passed on messages from Don, she included his mannerisms, so it was more like hearing the message in 3D. When she had Don 'on the line' for me, they would also share jokes together, as they would have in life! Melanie had also introduced us to Andy, also a dear friend to us and who was invaluable when Don died and a fitting channel for Don's first message two days after he died.

Christmas arrived on schedule, twenty-one days after Don had died. I had been warned that the first of everything was the worst, but Christmas was easier to get through than I expected. I think this was for two reasons. The first being that we all knew Don was with us, and the preparation for this Christmas had included Don, so he was an intrinsic part of the day. And, second, I know I was still in shock and I expect our children were the same. We were operating in 'safe mode'.

It was also made easier by the fact that I had presents for our children from their father, one of which had been ordered only five hours before he died. This made Don very much a part of that Christmas. He also had a seat at the table.

Our son, for Christmas, received two dog tags; one engraved with his own online squadron details and the other with Don's. This was significant because when Don was about seventy, he joined our son (and his platoon) in playing an online dog-fighting game that used fighter planes, with detailed specifications, from each country's air force in WWII. Although Don was decades older than the other players, and played less often, he nailed it and amassed quite a cache of planes.

There is almost fifty years between Don and Harley. The shared interest in dog fighting and Harley's pride in his dad's online dog-fighting achievements is beyond words. It was incredibly special that they had this connection. The dog tags celebrated and acknowledged this bond.

*Don's profile still comes up when Harley plays Warthunder.
He says he always takes his dad with him when he flies.
Don admired Winston Churchill hence the moniker he took on.*

For twenty-three years, Don and I worked together, organising one hundred exhibitions and shows. Don's call sign at events had been #1. The shows were also significant to Stacey while she was growing up. From sleeping under the desk as a baby to eventually selling tickets and working in the office, she loved and appreciated this unique lifestyle that her friends were so envious of. Don's present to our daughter was a Pandora #1 charm; a connection to her favourite childhood memories shared with him, and because she had always asked why we had a second child when we got it right the first time.

Our daughter had already experienced

Stacey and our Newfoundland, Buddha during setup of our 'Lifestyle' show in 1984.

intense grief when one of her best friends, Amanda, committed suicide when they were twenty-three. Their birthdays were one day apart. At times they fought like sisters. When Amanda committed suicide in New Zealand, Stacey was living in Sydney and we were living in Queensland. On the day we found out about her death, Don happened to be in Sydney for the day.

At one stage in my life I would have said that it was fortunate he was there, but I know now that this is exactly what happens in life. We are always being guided and looked after. Stacey didn't find out about Amanda's suicide until Don was there to support her. It was incredibly hard news for all of us, but especially for her to receive and she needed that support.

Amanda and Stacey were best friends from the first day of school. Two very smart little girls who were put up a class together within a couple of years. Amanda always had a smile, was sensible and capable. I would have said of all Stacey's high school friends, Amanda was the one most likely to succeed in life. We really don't know anyone's personal journey.

Stacey was devastated. With a lot of suicides, the people left behind wonder what they could have/should have done to prevent it. Everyone is on their own journey; I respect that Amanda took action from a depth of emotion that I had never experienced, until I lost Don, and then I understood.

At times, since Don died, I have felt a dark hopelessness and an appreciation of how intolerable life can be. Twenty-three days after Don died, Amanda's parents were in the country and Stacey was meeting up with them as she always did. I was reluctant. These people were friends of ours as well and I knew they knew grief as intimately as I did. Could I handle meeting people who carried grief as intense as mine? I felt I had enough trapped emotion in me, and if I added more, would I combust?

The interesting thing is that everyone had told me how to manage my grief because they had been 'there', but the words didn't resonate and, therefore, little comfort was received with the words. But when I met with these people, they said little, but spoke volumes. You don't need words when you are with people who truly understand; comfort is received but not through words.

Amanda had been gone for ten years but they still carried pain with them every day but hid most of it from others. We *never* stop loving and missing them, but the changes people see that satisfy them that we are 'getting on with life' is merely what we choose to let them see.

from my heart to yours...

Even after my experience, whenever I meet people who have lost a loved one, I don't know what to say to them. There are no words.

Because of your vulnerability, so much of what people say feels like it comes with judgement, especially if you sense that they expect you should have 'moved on'. Whatever that means.

If someone else gets 'over' their loss quicker than you do, it's probably not about technique but that the depth of the loss they suffered was not the same. But we are all different.

What can someone offer a person who is grieving? If you are going to ask, "How are you doing?" Change it to, "How are you doing *today*?" This then becomes an acknowledgment of the ongoing difficulty they are facing.

For me, it would be an opportunity to share stories about the person who has passed. They live on in conversation. Don made the world a better place.

Every life creates a ripple effect on everyone their life touches. Their presence on Earth is still felt regardless that they are no longer breathing the same air we are.

We need to continue to remember and value everyone we know who has ever walked this Earth. Too many stories are lost because we don't let new generations know what an amazing blood line they come from. We need to spend more time bringing wonderful memories and stories into the present. You will meet Ernest in the next chapter. He is a very nice man.

He walked into my heart like he always belonged there, took down my walls and lit my soul on fire.

T.M.

11

"Don, we need to talk"

29th December – twenty-five days after Don left this world

I had lights flickering every day and songs on the radio that I felt were a message, but from the time Don died, my daughter and I knew we would talk to Don through a medium. I'd had conversations with Don every day for thirty-seven years and I hadn't yet stopped talking to him, but our two-sided conversations had stopped. Talking to him again in a situation where I could hear his response couldn't come soon enough for me.

We chose Annette for the first reading because in a previous reading for our daughter, Amanda had come forward for the first time in ten years. We figured that if Annette could connect with someone who had never come forward before, it was likely she would have a good, strong connection with wherever Don was. Because of Christmas, the earliest we could schedule the reading was 29th December. The wait was agonising.

I have no doubt that mediums talk to the 'other side' but the urge to fill in gaps is strong. I try as much as possible to not volunteer information unless I am taking the conversation in the direction I want. I don't want to leave a session still having unanswered questions.

Anyway, I already know what I know, and I want to hear what they have to say so I try to leave the talking to them. In previous readings, I was specifically looking for guidance on where my life was heading and career opportunities, but this reading with Annette would be different. I needed to know it was Don I was communicating with, and then I had so many questions I wanted answered.

It was time to talk! I was so desperate to hear directly from Don that when we started the reading I couldn't speak; my emotions were just barely contained below the surface. I felt that if I opened my mouth all the anguish would pour out.

It had been twenty-five days since he had died. This was the longest we had ever been apart, ever! I was finally going to hear from Don; it was terrifying and exhilarating at the same time.

I sit down and Annette is shuffling tarot cards. She looks at me intently and her first words to me were about me selling the house. I shook my head and choked out the words that my husband had died at the beginning of the month. *'So, I suppose I will be selling.'* I know, I broke my own rule in record time.

She continued to look at me with an intensity and then asked what his first name was, then what his dad's name was and whether they were close. She explained that a *much older man* had stepped forward first, and that it usually takes a while after they have gone before they come into readings as they are not familiar with this process.

I asked, "What do you mean by much older?" I explained that Don was seventy-three. She apologised for assuming she would be looking for someone my age (That's comforting, I *felt* like I was a 70 year old!).

It's funny because people had not really seen or commented on our age difference, except at the beginning and then again at the very end.

Annette said, "Oh well, he's here straight away then."

I know I smiled at this statement. Of course, he would be ready and wanting to speak to me as well.

Annette reiterated that it usually takes a while after they have passed before they understand the process of coming into communication with the other side. I had always been confident he would be on the other side of any reading I scheduled, so I was glad (again) that I didn't understand this and delay scheduling the connection that I was so desperate for. I said, "I knew he wouldn't miss this meeting."

She advised, "Don is really peaceful and so he seems like someone who has been there a lot longer than just a few weeks. He's really peaceful." Aw, Don, exceeding expectations in the afterlife again.

Annette said, "He doesn't like missing out, does he?" I just smiled at that.

She went on to say, "Did he believe you keep on living on the other side?"

I said, "Yep." I had barely contained emotions that were keeping my responses to a minimum.

Annette said, "Because he's very much there, for someone who's just passed, that's why I thought he must be his dad."

I told her that we believed in past lives and already knew we'd had many lives together.

She confirmed that we had indeed had many lifetimes together and that he absolutely loved me dearly. I advised the feeling was mutual.

Don said, through Annette, "She has a lot of living to do and I don't want her to sit and vegetate."

Not what I expected. Damn it, Don! Your first words to me directly and you're telling me to get off the couch! Really? You are going to have to work on your communication skills.

Annette's reading continued, advising I would be okay, and that I would be selling the house. "Don's saying, 'It's just a house, even though it has so many memories.'" But I explained that this wasn't why I was reluctant to sell straight away. I knew I could only manage so much change at a time and I was still focused on just breathing my way through the intensity of grief. I didn't need the added stress of downsizing and selling.

Don also told me, "Just breathe and let yourself grieve. There is no timeframe on grief. You don't have to make any decisions right now. Don't rush into decisions. You are overwhelmed. There is some money coming. So, leave everything for a bit. Go through the grief period. Take it step by step and don't let anyone bully you into doing something. Lots of opinions will be given to you about what you should do. Everything will overwhelm you if you let it. Your focus needs to be on grieving, otherwise it will all come back on you."

I thought, *'This could be my Don, but... where's the personality?'*

Annette made a comment intimating that it would be difficult for me because Don would have made the decisions before (an assumption she made based on our age difference, I expect), but I advised it wasn't like that.

Then Don said (via Annette), "'Most of the time she made the decisions. I just agreed.' He said he liked to think he made the decisions, but he knows he didn't." Annette relayed what he said and then laughed and said, "What a character; he's so funny!" Now, I could see this was Don!

I realised I was smiling and felt happiness. Don always made me smile. This was the Don I knew. Here I was grieving, talking to him through someone else and it astounded me that he could still make me laugh and smile. That was crazy but priceless!

Don (via Annette), "He's saying, 'Everything will work out and I will be there around you, but I know it's not the same as being there with you.'"

She said Don pointed to his heart and acknowledged a broken heart. I'm sure this was to tell me he knew exactly what I was feeling. He was responding to my many ramblings about him being the only one who could truly understand what I was feeling in my heart. He was giving me acknowledgment of this.

Annette asked whether I knew Don's father as there was someone else there, but she didn't think it was his dad. Then she said, "It's his grandfather."

Wow! This was so unexpected. Don's grandfather, Ernest, had committed suicide when Don's dad was about nine. Don had *always* wanted to understand what had happened, but little was known or talked about. Despite this, Don felt a strong connection and empathy for his grandfather and always wished for more. Now he had the opportunity of a relationship. This was incredible.

Annette went on to say that Ernest had suffered severe depression throughout his life. He'd had an interesting journey, but it was not a good time at all, and it was too much for him.

She explained that during this reading he was fading in and out because suicide affects the soul. She said, "He's a very nice man."

She then went on to say, "Just letting you know it takes a lot of guts to commit suicide. You see some people attempt suicide and someone finds them, or it doesn't work. It just means it wasn't their time to go. Nobody gets to leave until it is their time to go, and there is an interesting energy around suicide because sometimes their soul goes into shock."

Annette then advised Ernest had piped in and said, "I'm all right."

Annette said to me, "They want to give you flowers. When you leave here, you have to buy and keep flowers around you, and they are from them." *'I will do this,'* I thought.

Annette asked *the significance of January/February*. I couldn't think of any birthdays or anniversaries in these months. This went back and forth; they kept reiterating this timeframe and I couldn't find a relevance. So, she went back to them to clarify why they were saying this was important. Annette looked fractionally annoyed and said, "Now they are just laughing." After the reading I worked this out and have added the details in *Significant bits* at the end of this chapter.

Annette then said, "I think Don would rather have gone than have health problems. If he survived the heart attack and was in hospital, he wouldn't have liked that at all. And *there is no full recovery from a heart attack at his age.*"

I said, "I knew he didn't want to suffer ill health, which was funny because I was a nurse when I met him, and he always said he married me so I could look after him in his old age. But he hasn't let me."

Annette advised, *"You already did."* I cried, as that was such an incredibly precious message to receive.

Then Annette said, "He wasn't a person to give up, but it was his time. He didn't give up."

This was significant because in my one-sided conversations with him, since his death, I had asked whether he would have stayed longer had his business been more of what he wanted. While in great pain and angry, I accused him of pulling out early because of work. When he was done with business, was he done with life? He was answering a question I had asked several times in the last twenty-five days. It was important to him that I understood that he hadn't given up!

I advised Annette, "Just prior to him dying I had cleared out old voicemails and I know there would have been ones where he said 'I love you', and it's really hard that I can't hear him anymore."

Annette said, "He says, 'I keep talking to you.'"

I asked, "Does he hear me talking all the time? When I'm upset or just when I'm happy? I thought they could only hear you when you are on the same frequency/good vibration."

Annette advised that needing to be on a happy frequency was further on down the track. Later he would step back a bit, but he would still be there. Then you will need to be upbeat to reach his frequency because he won't be able to get through the density of that (unhappy) emotion. He doesn't want to interfere in that process for you.

I was assuming he was saying he didn't want to interfere in the grieving process. Yeah well, he started it! But I have read somewhere that experiencing grief has a healing effect on the soul. I expect that when I truly understand that bit, it will be because I am also on the 'other side'.

I advised Annette that he was flickering lights at home and I wanted to understand what else he was doing.

She advised that loved ones find ways to communicate through lights, candles, tilting things like pictures, a breeze – either cool or a warmth when there's none. Eventually, Don may be able to knock (which can be annoying, she says). In bed you may feel someone is there. It is the only way they can communicate in the early stages of having passed.

Annette then showed me a soy candle that was for her brother who had been a missing person for about twenty-four years. However, she personally knew he had passed on about twenty years ago. She explained that the flame had caused the glass to go black, but it was soy and they don't go black. So, Annette had said to her brother, "Do you want to end this conversation? If you do blow the candle out then." He blew the candle out. Annette explained, "That's typical of him to do something dramatic." She advised that she still connects with him in dreams but not in the waking.

Annette asked whether Don and I had lost a baby. I said, "Yes, when Don was sixty-three and I was forty-six, we terminated a pregnancy." Annette said Don is letting you know *the soul of that baby is with Don now too* (this little soul is discussed in future readings as well; I had always thought it was an accident that I got pregnant but obviously not). I was starting to understand – there are no accidents.

Annette said, "Don's a lovely man, and everything will work out except that you can't get Don back. It's a hard time with your personal sadness, but it's a big growth time for you."

She asked me to give her a call in two months' time and she would give me the name of someone to communicate with Don through. She didn't believe I was ready for this yet (damn, must have been the bouts of crying throughout the session). She said, "This person doesn't do predictive readings. She communicates with those in spirit and just passes messages on. I know you are desperate for anything from him, but Don also must have his healing process, so we need to wait."

I wasn't sure how a reading with this other person would be different to what we'd just had, but I thought, *'That's okay, another conversation with Don to look forward to.'*

"Don, we need to talk"

Before Don died, we had come to understand that we'd had many lives together, but we didn't know any specifics. We understood that was why we were so comfortable with each other right from the start. I explained this to Annette, and she went on to say, "At some stage you lived in a situation where you were slaves or under some authority and that you were *kept apart*." (OMG!) "And, in this lifetime, you have been allowed to be together, well to Don's end in this physical world. You have had many, many lifetimes together."

Annette asked whether Don liked the water and then instructed me that when I am sad I should take myself to the lake or ocean and put my feet in the water and that I will feel him there.

I didn't realise that my earlier question, about how Don could communicate with us, was an answer from Annette, not Don. Don obviously wanted to respond himself, so he stealthily took Annette back to that question.

Annette said, "I see butterflies. Have you been seeing butterflies?"

"Yes," I said enthusiastically.

"That's him," she advised. Don had answered my question as he wanted me to know how he would be sending messages because he knew how important it was to me to receive them.

The reading had finished but then Don piped up again and said (via Annette), "Ring this lady in a couple of months and I will be there!"

I put a reminder in my phone to call Annette to get the contact information; however, I was worried that after this next meeting he could go 'out of reach'. In two months, he would have been gone three months, and she had indicated they can go out of reach after three months. This played on my mind. I was desperate for it but at the same time I didn't want to go in case it closed a door between us. Would that mean no more communication to look forward to?

There was so much to process from this meeting, and, of course, my comprehension was compromised by grief. It was invaluable to have a recording of it. Listening to it months later was like hearing it for the first time. Like re-watching an action-packed movie and picking up so much you had missed the first-time round. It was unbelievably precious to have this communication, and I kept reminding myself that Don had piped in at the end specifically to reinforce that he wanted this next meeting too.

I love him intensely. I know he still loves me. Love doesn't die.

The significant bits:

 Ernest's presence at the reading was significant. In hindsight, I am not surprised Don met up with his grandfather on the other side, but to bring him into the first reading was beyond any expectation, beyond perfect. Ernest had died in 1923, twenty years before Don was born.

Taken in 1902, this the only photo of Grandad Ernest Eade as an adult. He is holding Don's Uncle Roy. In those days, the stigma of a suicide impacted the whole family, so it is fortunate this photo was still in existence.

"Don, we need to talk"

This is the person Don was in life. He saw people, like his grandfather, and made sure they felt included and knew they were valued. Don wanted me to not just know he had connected with Ernest, but to introduce us, and he knew I would appreciate the significance of this. I was honoured.

Don wanted Ernest to know he was a special part of his family and therefore introduced him to his wife. It was beyond words. I cannot stress enough what an honour this was, and a testament to our relationship.

What did it mean to be dead if Don was behaving the same, doing the sort of things he would have had he been alive? It seemed irrefutable that it was only his body that had died. 'Don' was not his body; he was still here, and he was still Don.

The instruction to buy flowers was from both of them – this warmed my heart. I continue to do this, and, for some unknown reason, I tend to buy *yellow rosebuds.*

Ernest's presence wasn't mentioned again, but I believe it takes a lot of energy to be present in a reading and therefore he probably stayed for as long as he could. It was an honour to 'meet' him.

The significance of the January/February timeframe was lost on me during the reading because I was focused on birthdays or anniversaries. It was the laughter and knowing Don's sense of humour (still evident) that had me look outside the usual celebrations. I love that he shared this with his grandfather as well.

Before Don died, we had not discussed funerals or anything like that. He said he was going to do the ton (100 years) and I believed him, so we had plenty of time. Right? In my ramblings to him after he died, I told him that I was going to sprinkle his ashes from 'the boardwalk'.

Stacey was horrified years later to discover why we asked her to take this photo and why we wouldn't tell her what our private joke was.

This was a special place for us and maybe 'too much information' for some readers but we had discreetly engaged in an intimate act on the boardwalk of a well-known hotel chain multiple times over quite a few years. It was our secret. We were careful and never even came close to being caught. Nobody knew until after Don died when I had to explain that where I was sprinkling (some of) his ashes was personal. Nobody else could attend.

The relevance of the dates was that I had told Don (after death) that I would sprinkle his ashes off the boardwalk on Australia Day (26th January) or Valentine's Day (14th February). He obviously loved the idea and wanted me to know but wasn't prepared to share the 'details' with Annette, although he had with his granddad. What I loved about this was that I hadn't known how much of Don's personality remained. This was pure Don; his sense of humour and fun and chivalry were intact.

"Don, we need to talk"

♡ During the reading I had said, "I can't hear him say 'I love you' ever again." When I was transcribing this exact phrase from the recorded session for this book, I suddenly heard the radio downstairs. The actual lyrics came through loud and clear: 'I-I-I will always love you' belted out by Whitney Houston. There are times when I say something and get a response by song; this one was perfectly timed! He sent me an 'I love you'.

There are a lot of reasons why I credit Don with being a semi-silent co-author of this book, but after Whitney's song finished, the next song was one I had mentally said to myself, *'I need to remember what the 'I'm coming home' song was.'* That song played next, so I was able to get the details for a later chapter.

♡ Everything is said or happens for a reason. The relevance of the soul of the baby we didn't have, being with Don now, I didn't fully understand until fifteen months later. 'She' was also present in a few more readings before I understood.

♡ In a previous life together, we had been kept apart. Hearing this explained so much about our behaviour toward each other in this life. Finally, being allowed to be together explained our reluctance to be apart in this life and the feeling of desperation when we were.

When apart we would ring each other just to hear the other's voice. We would talk on the phone a minimum of three to four times a day, even if we were apart for just a day. Early in our relationship, I would cry when Don was away, and I knew it was 'over the top', even though I had a young baby at the time. I never understood why my reaction to his absence was so intense. Until this reading.

People usually fit into two categories with spirituality and speaking to the other side: you are either understanding of, or are curious and open to, spirituality and life after death, or adamantly against it.

So many people are on the fence or scared to have an opinion not shared by those around them, especially where religious instruction is to the contrary. That's okay. It doesn't require everyone to believe for it to exist.

I promise you, communication with a passed loved one is possible, and communicating with Don was the single most important step I took that enabled me to survive this horrendous event. He could not take the grieving away, *but he helped with my healing like no-one else could.*

Like a lot of people, psychic mediums were not part of our lives growing up. My first introduction to psychics was when our daughter was seventeen and living in another country on her own. We worried about her every day and had countless sleepless nights. Out of desperation one night I called a psychic hotline from an advert on TV.

The psychic told me my daughter was pregnant. I corrected her and told her no, my husband's daughter-in-law was pregnant. Two weeks later, our daughter came home because she was pregnant. I forgot all about that reading until years later.

I prefer to form an opinion on something only when I have enough unbiased information for it to become my belief. In 2004, Don and I were introduced to a psychic by a level-headed friend. We were astonished by the accuracy of the reading. This was real and we confidently added communication with the other side to our list of beliefs.

Don's mum had come into the first reading he had, but not in a convincing way. The personality described fitted her but there was no message that made it mind-blowing, it was just a 'hi'. I wonder whether it was frustrating for her to have waited so long before anyone 'left behind' was in a position for her to communicate with them. She had been a great communicator in life!

Please remember that I am telling you about my experiences. From my perspective, it's like making a phone call and 'they' need to answer the call. Don was always going to take a call from me, and I believe when you are calling out of love, there will be a connection when the time is right.

That said, I have reason to believe that if you carry any negative emotions about someone's passing, they feel this and may not answer or may not *be able* to answer. In a couple of situations I am aware of, it appears the spirits haven't come forward because of anticipated anger toward them; one was a suicide, the other chose not to have treatment.

It is my understanding that only love survives death and therefore love is the only vibration on the 'other side'. If you are not calling out of pure unconditional love, it's like tuning your radio to one frequency and expecting to hear what's being played on another. You are unlikely to be able to connect with the spirit.

I believe it works the same for communication from them to us. If we hold any negative emotions toward them or their death or to ourselves regarding their death like anger, regret, fear, shame, resentment, then we are unwittingly putting up a barrier they can't get through. They are light, they vibrate love. Negative emotions carry a weight and density they can't get through. It's heavy stuff. Let it go.

Also, this reading gave Don the opportunity to clarify something to me. He reiterated that, 'He wasn't a person to give up, but it was his time.' It was important to him that I understood this.

from my heart to yours...

Please understand that clairvoyants are human beings; therefore, there will inevitably be good ones and not-so-good ones. To put it in perspective, like builders, lawyers and priests, there are a small number of people who discredit their occupation, but the majority are good at what they do. If possible, go to someone who is recommended to you, or put it out there and look for the message.

Also know, on the other side, time does not exist, it's never too late, but sometimes you may try too early. You will get through when the time is right.

Generally, it is people who haven't had a reading that will tell you it's bogus. Do you want to take advice from someone who speaks from experience or someone who speaks from ignorance?

These people think that if the medium can't provide you with the lotto numbers then it's bogus. Clairvoyants are fed information from the spirit world that is intended to help us through life. It's only because we live in a material world that people think all they need is more money; they're just not looking deep enough. Whatever money they receive will never be enough because they are focused on the wrong thing. Their problem isn't money, they just don't know it yet.

So, communicating after death is an opportunity everyone has, and you don't need anybody else's agreement or approval. I've met people who have wanted to connect through a medium but have been more concerned with what people would think.

I had everyone talking to me about Don's death when the only one I wanted to hear from was Don. Something I would like you to consider is that your loved one probably wants to speak to you as well. I know Don did. As desperately as I did.

He wanted me to understand because he knew how much his death hurt me. He wanted an opportunity to explain and try to ease my pain.

Also, communication doesn't need to be through a medium. Don't hold on to assumptions or any unsaid apologies. Just do it, speak to them; they can and will hear you.

Some people think that because you are grieving you are vulnerable, but grief doesn't make you stupid, and you will know if you are talking to the person you knew so well.

Time is very slow for those who wait.
Very fast for those who are scared.
Very long for those who are lament.
Very short for those who celebrate.
But for those who love, time is eternal.

William Shakespeare

12

New Year's resolution – just survive

3rd January – one month after Don left this world

I went back to see Andy in January because my emotions where just out of control, and I knew I would come away feeling better. I was constantly looking for how I could feel at least a moment's relief.

I was lying on the massage bed in Andy's therapy room, and Andy told me Don was standing on my left. This was a treatment and not about having a conversation with Don so there wasn't a lot of dialogue. The main messages relayed were that he was there with me, and that he loved me, and that he had to go when he did. I was also told Don was learning to paint. I paint so I think he was doing it to connect with me, somehow. My eyes leak a lot, especially when I relax and am not holding myself tightly together, so my initial distress was evident. But I calmed; the meditative nature of the healing was soothing.

Near the end of the session, there was a light touch on my forehead that I would have thought nothing of except that when the session ended, Andy immediately told me how shocked he was that he had lightly kissed my forehead. It wasn't *him*. I knew this. I KNEW it was Don. I felt sorry for Andy.

Don used our connection through Andy to send me a very touching message. Andy is a dear friend that has always been professional. Don, however, was deeply committed to me and crossing boundaries was not new for him. *Deja vu*. I expect he probably got into trouble for 'crossing the line', even if it was just a stern word from Andy.

Don had (and obviously still has) a strong personality and his love for me was just as strong. It makes me smile just thinking about it. This was exactly what Don would do, kiss my forehead, and obviously being dead was not going to be a barrier when the force was strong. Yep, that's my Don, it was not Andy.

I was intrigued, but not surprised, that Don could channel his love and determination and deliver a message in a way that I would have considered impossible but would know was from him. *Maybe I should take up pottery!*

But love is the strongest of emotions. Poor Andy, this had never happened before, and he'd been doing this for a long time. In my head I could hear Frank Sinatra singing 'I did it my way'.

I have since read that kissing someone on the forehead, in the third-eye area, brings a sense of security and wellbeing. Aw, Don. There was no denying this was my Don, and our connection was strong.

Because I knew Don could use the lights, I turned them on whenever I was at home. And every time I was there, Don flickered the lights, mainly in the kitchen because this was the heart and centre of the house and I was always in there. This was perfect because it meant the next time our son was with me at home, the lights started flickering and he could not deny this evidence of his dad's continued presence in our lives. He had been reluctant to accept this until he experienced it.

Sometimes when Don flickered the lights, I knew he was responding to something I had said; other times, he may have sensed the need to reassure me of his presence, or he just wanted me to know that he was with me and I wasn't alone.

In life, Don had always anticipated my state of mind and provided quiet support with just his timely presence, a look, a cup of tea placed quietly in front of me or, most often, a hug. The hugs are one of the things I miss the most. There was a hug for every occasion.

We were then more open to messages from Don. I don't recall when the butterflies started, but Don confirmed through Annette in the December reading that he was sending us butterflies.

A big brown, white and black butterfly would come and dance around me in the backyard then leave. Stacey had also been seeing these brown 'friendly' butterflies at her house.

Then I started getting the most beautiful vibrant-blue butterfly in the garden outside my home office window. I tried catching it on camera, but it was too quick, or it was too tiny with fluttering wings to capture on film from the distance I was taking the photo from.

Our daughter, the recipient of only brown butterflies, wanted to know what type the blue one was. I told Don he would have to keep the butterfly there longer so I could get a photo. And he did! The next time it came it landed on a branch and I rushed to get my phone. I was able to photograph it because it just stayed on the leaf. After the quick photo session, it flew away. Sure, it was behaving like any other butterfly but that was the only time it stayed, and it was after I had asked for an opportunity to photograph it. I then identified it as a blue morpho. These ones were special to me. I was the only one who received the blue butterflies from Don. Stacey gave me a necklace with a vibrant-blue morpho wing preserved inside it from a butterfly sanctuary in North Queensland. This was why she needed to know what the butterfly was.

I was also made aware that feathers in your path are a message left from the other side, and I received a lot of feathers from

Don. I picked up most of them but there was no requirement to pick them up. The message has been received when you see the feather.

Regardless of how much I was suffering, I felt deep appreciation for being left messages of love. A few times, the timing, quantity or type of feather made the gift even more memorable. My favourite feather gift was the one I received on 29th January.

I had just finished coffee at one of my usual cafés and was opening the car door while talking to my daughter on the phone. Out of the corner of my eye I saw a feather slowly floating down toward me. I stood and stared in wonder. I lifted my arm, opened my hand and it floated onto my palm. It was handed to me! The feather was different. It was beautiful, and the incredible thing was that Don handed it to me from the other side.

The feather is now attached to Don's photo on my desk and reminds me of this incredible happening every time I want to focus, not on my loss but on what I can never lose, our love.

Don also started to send messages via music, mainly, but not exclusively, through the radio.

Before Don died, I didn't like extra noise in the house. It was peaceful without the radio plus I could always

This feather was an expression of pure love and was an incredibly special post-death experience we shared.

hear Don somewhere in the house (especially when he was doing the dishes; I'm sure the neighbours heard him when he was doing the dishes).

After he died, I needed the radio playing in the background to take away some of the emptiness in the air. However, because I was working from home and spending a lot of time on teleconferences, it meant the radio couldn't be loud enough to be heard through the phone.

The first time I received a lyric-based message from Don, I was working in the office. Some lyrics came through louder and clearer than the rest of the song had been. I was nowhere near the radio. There was no-one else in the house. The words heard clearly were about me being the reason and the depths he would go to, to be with me. I left my desk and went to the radio. I knew he had played it and it was a message.

Don had regularly commented on my ability to truly focus when I was working; he would put a cup of tea in front of me and I wouldn't be aware of it happening. So, for lyrics to get through to me meant something, especially given the radio volume was deliberately low.

Another set of lyrics that stood out were from 'Everything I do' by Brian Adams. I believe he used specific words to get my attention and that the whole song was a message. I particularly liked the suggestion that I would find him by looking into my heart and soul. Yes, that's where my Don is now.

The song that Don played the most and that held special meaning was 'Perfect' by Ed Sheeran and Beyoncé. So many of the lyrics resonated with when we had first met and married. This particular song referenced dancing and I didn't like dancing so Don had a 'work-around' – he would hug me and sway while he hummed. We used to take a blanket into the backyard and 'sway' on the grass, then lay down and discuss the day.

This was now 'our song'. It was a popular song at the time but the timing of when it was played was sometimes beyond coincidence. At times, I really needed him to tell me he was there. I would be needing his support and the song would start. Every time it played on the radio I went and stood at the photo wall with my hand on the photo where his heart was, and tears streamed down my face. I felt closer to him. The song brought our hearts to the same space.

He also played this song when I was out of the house. Two times stand out. A previous colleague and good friend offered me a job after Don died. I questioned whether life was directing me toward this person; why else had he come into my life, why else was I being offered a new job? I arranged to meet him and discuss the position.

We were having dinner in a restaurant, but I wasn't saying much. Then, 'Perfect' started playing. I had heard no music in the restaurant up until this point, so I asked whether they had karaoke. This would have explained why this song was playing all of a sudden. But no karaoke. My friend no doubt thought I had an interest in Karaoke – yikes – ahh no! Did Don play that song with volume and clarity so I would hear it and know he was there? When I got the opportunity, I was going to ask Don whether he played the song and why.

Another incidence was when our daughter, son-in-law and I went to Brisbane for her birthday. Getting ahead of myself here, but this was six months after Don died, and her birthday was always a big deal for her even though she had to share it with her brother (but that's another story). She was close to her dad and this was her first birthday without him. We parked in the wrong place, walked miles, had a drink at another bar and eventually found the restaurant. When we finally walked in, a local singer had started singing 'Perfect'. It was Don saying he was there with us for this celebration.

One night I said to Don that I missed not hearing him say 'I love you'. I had heard it repeatedly for decades and it had been his last words to me; now nothing. In the morning I went downstairs, turned the radio on and the first lyrics to play held a message that all the times when he told me he loved me, he was also telling me he would love me forever. Such a beautiful message to receive.

With lyrics, a change in volume and clarity made them unmissable. It was a relief when I was later advised that Don put his energy into things like music. This made sense as to why it reached out to me. I stopped second-guessing whether there was a message from him. If it felt like a message, it was, and most often the songs were well-timed, on-point and perfect.

So many nights when I went to bed, I asked Don to come into my dreams. If he couldn't get any closer to me, maybe I could get closer to him. I understand everyone dreams, but I am one of those who never remembers dreaming. Don has come into other family members' dreams with a vivid presence and leaving the recipient feeling his strong love for them. They reported that he appeared so real, not like a dream.

I want to believe he comes into my dreams, but that I am not supposed to remember them, otherwise I would. I have only come close to remembering a dream once and it was like I caught the tail end of it before being fully awake. I was walking through a field of daisies and was laughing and looking back saying, "I'm going to have to plant some daisies now."

from my heart to yours . . .

I remember early in our relationship I went for a week's holiday to my grandparents in the South Island of New Zealand. I needed a break, not from Don, but from the constant criticism and negativity about our relationship. Even early in the relationship, separation was difficult for us and Don would ring and say, "I just wanted to hear your voice." Sometimes, the smallest of messages is all you need. So many of my messages from Don were small; they were just big deals to me. A feather on my path, the lyrics being sung when I turned on the radio...

I know I am not the only one receiving messages. I worked with someone who shared this story with me. A friend of hers had died years earlier. He had a classic car that he loved. One day at the traffic lights, a song that reminded her of him played on the radio. She looked up and there was a car just like his. He was saying, *'I'm here.'* It was merely an acknowledgment of their ongoing connection.

If you are open, and pay attention, you are more likely to receive your messages.

We are never really alone.

Grief is love,
and excruciating pain,
but I would not trade
a moment of my grief
for a life less loved.

Pam Eade

13

Grief is love!

11th January - one month, 8 days after Don left this world

I was fortunate in that my employer was incredibly supportive during this time. To pay for the holiday that never was, I had put in a request to have accumulated leave paid out. For some reason it wasn't processed, but then a week later I was asking for it to pay for Don's funeral. I know I didn't have enough payout to cover the funeral, but they paid me the full amount I needed anyway. They were there for me in ways I didn't expect.

From the CEO to colleagues, associates and my team, the outpouring of support, texts and emails were heart-warming and sincere. Another part of the support they gave me was access to a grief counsellor. I probably would not have looked at this option myself, but it ended up being extremely helpful and much appreciated.

My first session was booked for 11th January, and I trusted that the person assigned to me would be the right fit, and he was. I never met George as our sessions were by phone, but he appreciated my beliefs, so our conversations were relevant for me.

The times I felt most connected to Don was when I was talking about him, so it was great to be able to tell a new person what a wonderful man and relationship I had lost.

George also gave me an anchor. I suddenly understood what I was going through and why it was so hard. George's words clarified my grief perfectly:

"Grief is love."

OMG. I got it. I understand completely. I can do this because my grief *is* going to be horrendous. It *will be* unbearable. It *will* break me and all because I loved this man and was loved in return with an intensity that not everyone gets to experience in this lifetime. These words represented the following to me:

 Grief is love

Love I understand, and it made sense that the intensity of my grief was relative to the intensity of the love I had 'lost'. From my perspective, I knew *I would not trade a moment of my grief for a life less loved.*

 Grief is love

These three words gave me the power I needed to grieve on *my* terms. The relationship I had with Don was ours alone. It was between Don and me and it didn't matter what others thought I should do. This was 100 percent *my* grief. I owned it along with the processes that helped me get out of bed, or not.

 Grief is love

It is my belief that we each have a specific amount of love in us for every individual we know. You may try to love someone more or love them less, but it is what it is for each individual. This love converts, in equal proportion, to grief when they die.

When I became overwhelmed by grief and my thoughts were in turmoil, when reality was warped, and my rationale was shaky, these words didn't ever feel false. This was my lifeline because its logic was unbreakable. They gave me balance and perspective.

I will grieve my loss until I die, but I do believe the releasing of grief from my body is finite, and that the more I let it flow out, the sooner that part of grieving will be done. I cried every day for over twenty-two months. The tears didn't stop after that, but it was the end of the streak where for approximately six hundred and seventy days I had cried without missing a day. This was longer than I expected – far longer than people advised it would take – but that was okay because it was a conversion of love.

George also helped me with two specific issues while in my weakened state. Prior to the loss, I would have been able to handle these problems easily. One was to get a 'friend', who I then saw as predatory, out of my life. George helped me decide what I needed to do, what I needed to say, how to deliver the message and how to protect myself from future communication.

I also discussed with George an issue I was having with a telecommunications company who would not shift my mobile number from Don's account into my name without talking to Don first. This went on for *four months* with me fearing my phone would be cut off because Don was no longer paying his bill. Every time I rang to discuss it, they asked me to put Don on the line. Every time! I feared calling them to sort it out and I feared not calling them and having my phone disconnected. They disconnected my phone twice. While on one of our calls, George initiated and completed a complaint to the telecommunications ombudsman on my behalf. The issue was resolved within a week.

In a previous chapter, I mentioned how Don sent me a kiss through someone else. Another channelling was with the grief counsellor. During one of the phone sessions, I explained that I had run out of the herbal supplement for stress because I couldn't get to the naturopath during working hours.

George said, "I have this incredibly strong urge to get up now and go straight there and get it for you." I laughed. George was surprised by his own reaction, but this was classic Don. He would have done this in life and if he could get someone else to do it in his absence, he would. George mentioned several times how strong the feeling was and how uncharacteristic that was for him. I don't even know whether George and I were in the same city, I expect we weren't.

George also advised me to write a journal and then later to add a gratitude page. Journaling ended up being one of the most important self-care tools I used. It helped me release so much heavy emotion, and it gave me perspective on how far I had come when at times I looked back on past entries. The gratitude part helped me appreciate the good bits in my life that I would have taken for granted had I not been noting their existence.

from my heart to yours...

The sessions I had with George were invaluable, mainly because I could talk openly to him and his responses always resonated with me, and he didn't seem to tire of me talking about Don.

He listened. He didn't judge. I enjoyed the sessions because I could speak freely, and I wanted desperately to talk about Don.

Helping me with issues I was struggling to deal with myself were invaluable. Creating a habit of journaling and writing a gratitude page has helped me in a way that exceeds that of grief management. I will forever be grateful for this opportunity, given to me by my work, and for George himself.

Twelve months after my sessions with George stopped, I had another grief counsellor that wasn't a 'George' and I felt

I gained nothing from the sessions. This counsellor seemed to be following prescribed techniques and dialogue and nothing resonated. Make sure that if you are talking to someone, they make you feel you are in a safe and supported space. Don't persevere with someone who is not a good match, irrespective of whether they're a trained counsellor, friend or family member. Find someone else. If you are going to do it, do it right. This needs to be what works best for you.

We can complain because rose bushes have thorns, or rejoice because thorn bushes have roses.

Abraham Lincoln

14

"If I write down my thoughts, will I sound crazy?"

19th January – one month, fifteen days after Don left this world

The first journal I started was seven weeks after Don died. My intention was that I would 'get it all out' about losing Don in the first journal, and the second journal would be about me. To a strategic planner that made sense. But the reality was that twenty-three months and six journals later, Don was still featuring. From the sixth journal though he was mainly as gratitude in my daily entries.

I was new to this death business and some unexpected events occurred, so journaling was a good opportunity to celebrate the nice unique experiences as well as purging heavy emotion from my mind/body.

Journaling was undoubtedly one of the most important tools I had. It was a way of processing my grief. I wrote in the journal in bed. Sometimes I wrote in it during the day but would always ensure it was also the last thing I did at night. This enabled me to empty my brain as much as possible so I could fall sleep.

The following is a compilation of some of my early entries, either the entry itself or a summary of what I wrote at the time.

My first entry was addressed to Don.

19th January 2018

Dear Don, it has been 46 days, 5 hours and 14 minutes since you rocked my world in the worst possible way. I grieve my loss with an intensity few would understand – probably only you. After a lifetime of fixing problems together and bouncing back quickly from every challenge, I am now faced with the impossible.

This problem cannot be fixed or painted pretty, and I am alone.

25th January 2018

I am paralysed by grief and that's okay. Everyone says they understand, but at some point they have an expectation that I will be 'better' or 'getting back to normal'.

It is so hard knowing I will have to function without him and feeling I shouldn't be able to. It's not the guilt of moving forward, it's more like a resistance to be snipping away any of the threads that keep us attached.

The death/grief process is rife with contradictions. I can't believe he has been gone for 7 weeks and yet I know he has not been here for 7 weeks – we have never been apart this long. I know it's too hard to manage without him, but reality says **I already am!**

The most liberating thing I heard was that grief is love. My love for Don is evident to everyone so my grief should be allowed the same freedom.

Why do people decide how others should grieve when it is so deeply personal, and no two experiences can ever be the same? They wouldn't riffle through my underwear drawer but think they have a right to review my most personal crisis and pass judgement.

"If I write down my thoughts, will I sound crazy?"

In February I noted that I was having flashbacks. Memories would flash into my mind. They were random and vivid and the emotions I felt were intense, like experiencing it all over again. They were all good, heart-warming memories. I believed Don or my subconscious or both were balancing my pain with memories that generated good feelings. Reinforcing that what I had lost was something incredibly valuable. In reality, I hadn't lost anything. I still had these as memories when he was alive, but I have a new appreciation for them now.

The memories are not significant events, but I can look back on the past and feel how blessed I was. There is not a memory where I didn't feel loved and supported. Is this what people with forms of dementia experience? Reliving the past in their minds? It is a beautiful place to be when the present is full of pain. Maybe I was drowning in grief and my life was flashing before my eyes (eyeroll).

It was also at this point where I started to be impatient with the grieving, mainly because it was not happening like I was told it would, and I wanted it to, badly. Was I doing something that was making this harder for me?

I was mourning the loss of who I was. I wanted to be the me I was with Don. I didn't know myself anymore. I was trying to fill a void, but it was impossible to substitute 'us'. I was lost. This feeling was directing me on what I needed to do to move forward. I needed to find the Pam that was not part of 'us', I just wasn't sure there was one. I was confused. I was conflicted.

I went back to work, but it wasn't easy. I started feeling anger. I had a business trip coming up and I knew I would have to appear normal and balanced. On the morning I arrived in Sydney for the meeting, I found the telecommunications company had disconnected my phone. This was so unfair. An hour before my meeting, I was crying on the phone because they wanted me to put my husband on the phone again. This person assured me it wouldn't ever happen again. I had heard that before, in every conversation when they finally grasped the insensitivity of their incompetence. In all cases, the previous conversations were there in front of them, they just hadn't read them. Needless to say, my phone was reconnected immediately; however, that wasn't yet the end of their requests to speak to Don.

The (beep beep) washing machine was just another problem and a constant reminder of the depth I had sunk to. I couldn't even do my own washing. I was so angry.

The washing machine was given to Don by someone whom I felt used him and took advantage of his kind nature. After Don died, I realised I had never used this washing machine. It was a front loader. It stopped washing mid-cycle and I couldn't get my clothes out. I didn't even know how to use that piece of shit. I kicked the shit out of it and screamed to Don to get his butt back here and take care of the bloody thing. This was his responsibility! Of course, he didn't show up. Maybe because of the unprecedented colourful language (which I have toned down here using poetic licence).

I didn't get any divine intervention or inspiration on what to do, or maybe I did; I called a repairman. I don't know whether that was good or not, whether the repair fee was more than the machine was worth. I was so angry. This was my angriest moment and was not witnessed or discussed with anyone, but I was still ashamed of my outburst. I mention this because I know it is an unwelcome 'stage of grief', but this outburst also has a significance later.

At this stage I was so tired of the constant challenges that seemed never-ending, and that I was dealing with on my own. This was the first time in my life I had an appreciation of why people commit suicide. I thought, *'I.DON'T.WANT.TO.LIVE.'*

"If I write down my thoughts, will I sound crazy?"

I had already decided there was a specific amount of grief attached to Don that I had to release. There were no short cuts. You need to release it all or it becomes hardened and is held as anger or pain. So, I promised myself to cry as much and as deeply and as often as I needed to with no self-judgement or negative self-talk.

On 8th February I started writing a gratitude page as part of my nightly journaling. This was incredibly hard, but under a deep layer of grief I knew I had a good life. I had much to be grateful for and I wanted some balance in my life. I had lived a life of mostly laughter and fun because we never allowed ourselves to give in to the bad times for long.

It was easier than I expected to find things to be grateful for because I was determined to do my 'homework'. My initial motivation wasn't optimal, but it got me going and then it became easier to see the blessings in my life. I was grateful for green trees and sunshine, for butterflies, for friends and coffee, for green lights and parking spaces, for a life lived in love, for my job, my house, for Winnie the cat.

I also had good days because I was determined to use every tool available to me to rise above the grief. And when I felt really sad, I rang someone I knew I would be able to laugh with. The analytical side of me was looking for triggers and also coping mechanisms.

I recognised I was suffering from depression, so I went to my naturopath. I'm not a health nut but am conscious of my health. I listen to my body and act early rather than waiting for issues to escalate. To avoid visits to the doctor or dentist, I'll engage in whatever preventative measures I can to avoid them. I know stress affects the body. It depletes essential vitamins and minerals that need to be replaced in order to function optimally. I knew I needed to top up what had been depleted so I could cope with the next load of stress that was on its way.

All of this does not take away my grief and sadness, and nothing can make it emotionally okay that Don is gone. But it is so easy to blame every emotion I have on grief when, in reality, before Don died, times in my life had sucked. This wasn't the first time in my life I had cried.

I had a lot of tools I could use to, in part, counter the inevitable dips on the rollercoaster that was my life. These, in turn, gave me a sense of having regained some of my strength and self-determination.

Grief brought up insecurities and fears and bundled them all together. I wailed on how I needed Don's advice, to hear his words, when really I hadn't before he had died. I had always been good at making decisions, but I created more loss by telling myself I needed Don for this.

I was creating chaos in my head. It is undeniably harder to make even simple decisions while grieving; everything feels too hard, but people give you space and time. My confusion came through in the journaling. I was trying to analyse how to manage my grief instead of just accepting it. But I was trying to find my way through.

I knew the things that made me cry so I did them deliberately as I just wanted to get it all out and be able to function normally. I looked at photos at night in bed, the video of his life from the funeral, and I played the songs I knew he played for me on the radio. Surely, the quickest way through grief to the calm I was seeking was to release, release, release.

I knew what was making me happy. I put together a movie of photos of us, particularly anniversary photos, so I could put the memory on Facebook.

I was also managing my public persona at this time. I compartmentalised my grief so I could function in public. I knew my love for Don was in every breath I drew and every beat of my heart. I realised that the challenges I had faced previously in my life were superficial in comparison.

I made a list of what I had lost and what I had gained.

Lost: my soul mate, lover, best friend, husband, sense of my own strength, perceived purpose in life. It felt like I had lost everything.

Gained: freedom (hadn't realised I didn't have this before), self-determination (I thought I already had this), a new purpose (defining who I was), independence (not seeing the upside, but maybe later).

I saw the following little story and it resonated with where I was at this time, as it cleverly put choices in perspective:

A wise old lady is boiling carrots, eggs and coffee in separate pots of water. She asks, 'What do you want to be?'

Carrots, although they start off hard become soft.

Eggs, although they start off fragile and soft, they become hard.

Coffee changes the water and becomes better.

Me, I was choosing to be coffee!

By March, I had built a list of self-help tasks so that the moment I felt my life was outside my control, I ticked off some of the easier things. Deep breathing was an easy one to do. The list was my survival toolkit and I have reproduced it in Part IV. Trust me, I did actually do this. Every day I made a list that included super-easy and more difficult items with a checkbox beside each one. It gave me a clearer plan for the day and a sense of achievement at night.

Acceptance was an important item. I did accept this was an incredibly painful event in my life and no amount of meditation, breathing, water or journaling would heal what ailed me so soon after Don's death.

Even so, I still had the worst stretch of days and was beside myself with grief, loneliness and helplessness. When I needed something more, I reached out to people I knew, and the amount of love that came back to me was like a tsunami. I would have a relatively good day followed by a really bad one. At least when I had a bad one, I could tell myself there was another good one coming. And my expectation was that even though a bad one was inevitable; the good days would become progressively longer.

During this time, I was also getting messages of support from Don. On one particular day, I was writing in my journal, trying to get stuff out of my head so I could move. There was tapping behind me and I found a big brown butterfly on the window, trying to get *out*. I had to catch it and set it free. Then I questioned why this happened and the relevance of the timing.

I googled and found: *'The brown butterfly symbolises new life/a fresh start, and being in the house can mean the actual soul of a deceased loved one is there.'* 'I'll take it,' I thought, *'Don's reading what I'm writing and sends me love – thanks Don! I needed that!'*

So, this was a period where I focused on gratitude and attitude.

I deliberately said 'thank you', either in my head or out loud, when I saw or experienced something that was good, like birds flying in front or alongside me when I was driving (like dolphins do with boats). I said thank you when I found a feather on my path, especially when I had gone off the path. A song from Don, thank you. A butterfly, thank you. Appreciating a cool breeze on a hot day, thank you. A bird singing nearby, thank you. Every green light I got to drive straight through, thank you. Getting a parking space, thank you. The items on my shopping list that were on special, thank you…

"If I write down my thoughts, will I sound crazy?"

The worst part of the day was late afternoon/evening, as for thirty-plus years this was our companionship peak of the day. We would be discussing our day and preparing to share a meal. So now, at this time, it would be so easy to think my whole day/life was crap and that nothing good had happened, but I knew during the day I had said thanks for an abundance of seemingly small things, easily forgotten when I felt low.

Don and I had many situations where we held a different view without the other being wrong. We were individual thinkers after all, and you can't claim to be both individual thinkers if you always have to agree. Our life was full of random, fun conversations where we had opposing views. Here's an example:

What is your body saying to you when you feel hungry?

Don believed hunger was his body telling him he needed to eat.

Pam believed hunger was her body saying, 'Yay, my metabolism is working.'

Neither of us were wrong. Don had lived during a time when food had been in short supply. I hadn't. We had different perspectives, that's all. Guess which one of us didn't have a weight problem? Just saying. I also know I'm in the minority with my view because all the fast-food companies are on Don's side. They're forefront in conditioning a mentality that if you are hungry before dinner, you don't just snack, you have a meal! Regardless, having differing views was part of the fun with our random inane conversations and is one of the things I miss the most.

Our attitude to life was the same though, and we were both very much coffee people! We also had a strong view that we could and would overcome all obstacles and turn a challenge into a good thing. "Only good will come of this." was our catch phrase. So, it did.

I knew I would have to have a good life after the worst of the grieving was done, otherwise what was the point. I would make sure there was a point to being here and suffering as I had.

My brain wanted to make this a process based on logic.

My heart knew a different reality. This was about love.

My soul knew this was a transformation for my human side so I would come to the realisation that we were never apart.

The reality was, it just was, and it would hurt.

I had felt cherished for so long; I couldn't comprehend life without so much love in it. This was not a one-sided contract. I know I helped Don immensely on his journey but that was his story. We all have our own story to tell.

In this chapter, Don had been gone for two to four months and it was a rollercoaster. Some of my thoughts may resonate with you and you will know you are not alone.

I believed gratitude and attitude were particularly important in my life at this time.

While in business in New Zealand in the late 1980s, Don was asked why our (marketing and promotion) business was *growing* during a recession. He said, "Because we choose not to participate."

I reminded myself of this so I could move towards that mode of thinking again and create a life for myself that flowed.

from my heart to yours...

Gratitude and attitude. When my mood took a dip, I looked within and focused on whatever felt lacking and I worked on that. I tried not to focus on what was *not* in my life to the point that I forgot to appreciate the good that was here, right now.

I highly recommend the journaling as it was essential for me to unload at the end of each day. I felt I was constantly releasing emotions and therefore wasn't accumulating bad energy that could fester. Looking back, I was able to see that the entries reflected my emotions going up and down and the immense pain I experienced for an interminable period of time.

The only upside of this time was looking back on it! I liked this position better. It meant I had, in fact, survived worse pain than I was currently experiencing. I felt deep sorrow for the me I was at that time but could see I was no longer her. I may not have felt strong, but I was definitely stronger than I was. Sometimes, it felt like nothing had changed, and you wonder when it will end. The journal gives you perspective. You can see you are in a better place, even though it's not the best place, yet.

It took over two years before I stopped feeling the need to journal before sleep; however, I have no intention to ever stop the gratitude page. It is an uplifting feeling being grateful. It can be uplifting at the end of the day, regardless of the day you have had.

Know that it is only you who chooses what you think. It is always your choice. No-one is in your head but you.

They who we love and
lose are no longer where
they were before.
They are now...
wherever we are

Unknown

15

The much-anticipated talk with Don

17th March – three months, thirteen days since Don left this world

Don had now been gone for three and a half months. In the leadup to my second opportunity to chat with him I was so distraught. So much was going on in my head. I wanted to accept his death but really all I was looking for was a way for Don to not be gone. I wasn't ready! Funnily enough, the day before he died, I was more ready (as in stronger, more independent) than I was after he died.

At the time of the reading I was excessively emotional. PMT? Probably. The healing new moon that brings out our innermost fears (I read this somewhere)? Possibly. Crap times that just go on and on and on? Yep, that too! I was a mess.

I was preparing myself for the reading that I was told to schedule at this time. It felt more like a high-pressure business meeting than a reading. This was not me, but, at the same time, it was the only me who was available at the time. I had panic attacks about the reading. Why? Because I had a real fear that Don would cease to be available to me after this reading, because of the three-month timeframe advised by Annette. I was worried that having this reading would allow him to 'move on' and be out of my reach. I needed him to be there at least until I got myself together.

The time preceding the meeting with Rouna was torture. My daughter and I arrived early and sat in the car around the corner from her house. I was suffering anxiety and wasn't sure I could go through with it. My thinking was that if I didn't go ahead with this session, would he have to stay contactable for longer? But although I had suffered grief intensely since Don died, there had been periods where I was okay. These random periods of calm showed me that I would eventually be in a good place. But when?

I have a recollection of a butterfly beside us, which we both saw as Don being there and saying, *'Don't worry, I'm with you.'*

Between the session with Annette on 29th December and this meeting with Rouna on 17th March, I had contacted a tarot reader in Nimbin. She had given me a reading about ten months *before* Don died that had been really interesting, but also had a significant relevance to where I was following his death.

In early March, I had called the tarot reader and requested a reading over the phone. She was not a friendly person, but I felt desperate for something. This wasn't about contacting Don; it was for me to get a sense of what lay ahead in my life. During the call she offered to bring Don 'in', and I quickly said, "No, I already have a session booked to talk to him." She was not the sort of person I wanted managing a conversation between Don and me.

I had never met Rouna before this. I wasn't sure what to expect but she was recommended, so I was going where I was being led. It was a long session, and, for clarity, I have written relevant parts verbatim and other parts are summarised. The session was recorded.

Rouna started by immediately asking about yellow roses. "What is it with yellow roses?"

I explained that I felt Don liked them. They were on his casket with sunflowers but also, as per Don and Grandad Ernest's instructions, I was buying flowers (from them) and most often I had yellow rosebuds on the kitchen counter.

Rouna said, "That's funny. I was talking to my husband this morning about how pretty our *one red rose* in the garden was. The petals had all fallen on the grass, but someone had already started in my head today saying, 'No, it's yellow roses' and kept on at me about them. And now the first thing that comes through is yellow roses."

Then she said, "Okay, there's no hesitation about him being here, he's right here. Pam, please don't worry about how much you cry and what you go through because it's really important he gets to tell you these things." (Rouna thought she was giving me permission to cry. Hah! There was actually no chance I wouldn't be bawling; crying was the least I would do.)

Rouna was actually crying herself at this stage and was recounting what Don was saying. "The first thing he's saying to you is, 'I prepared you for everything in your life except me leaving,' and he said, 'And I should have prepared you for my loss.'"

Rouna said, "I need to tell you I'm really strong when *you* cry, I'm your strength, but if *they* cry, I cry, and the tears are streaming down Don's face."

I see him in my mind and this image of him breaks my heart. I had always wondered whether Don felt our separation as strongly as I had. This was confirmation. He was as emotional about our separation as I was. I knew he would have been emotional about it in life, now I knew it was the same in death.

Rouna said, "He says, 'Don't worry about the children, they are getting the support they need.' He worries about you. He says, 'Stop listening to everyone telling you what to do.' He's saying to you, 'Do what's in your heart. The journal is probably the best thing that you have ever started doing, write it, and read.' There is something he wants you to read that's going to give you peace. He's saying you don't read much."

I said, "I read *all the time,* but I like romance suspense mysteries. I have the Deepak Chopra book about life after death though."

Rouna laughed and said, "Don is saying you read but, in his opinion, you don't read because you read those novels. There is one thing you should be reading. *It is not the answer to all*, but it will give you some peace. You picked up the Deepak Chopra book about life after death recently and there was a reason he guided you to that. And he's saying again, 'You don't really read' (and he laughs)."

Rouna asked if there was something about crosswords, "Were they something he liked, or you liked?"

I explained, "There's a word game we did together in bed just about every night. I still do it because I feel connected to him when I do. We used to come up with answers together. I actually sensed that he's there because *I come up with words I don't even know*, so I was sure he was beside me helping. Also, if I was on my own, it should be taking me twice as long, but it's taking the same time or less than when we were both doing it together."

Rouna confirmed he was talking into my right ear, and she said, "That's amazing."

Rouna advised that he was going back to the journals. "Somebody is in your head saying you shouldn't be doing it. Don't listen to them. And don't allocate an amount of time for grief, don't allocate a time period for missing me because *it's about the heart; it's got nothing to do with time*. It's really, really important you understand that."

We then moved on to talking about his actual death. Rouna said she saw blood running out really quickly. I advised he died suddenly of a heart attack. She asked whether there was history of high cholesterol in the family and whether someone else had experienced heart cholesterol problems. I confirmed this would be Don's mum.

"Don is saying, 'Nothing could have prevented this,' and that's really, really important to him. *He wants you to know he didn't want to leave you, but he had to go.*"

Rouna asked whether he died in hospital because he was showing her a hospital bed. She was mumbling to Don, "Why are you showing me a hospital bed, come on, tell me. Come on, Don, tell me what the hospital bed is about?"

She said she was seeing the bed and he was there, "And I'm seeing the hospital and he's not talking to me. He doesn't even want to answer me when I say that."

Of course, I could only hear Rouna, but I sensed what was happening with Don and was sure I could feel his anguish. The fact he wasn't speaking spoke volumes. I advised Rouna, "He had previously shown the hospital bed, and I knew he had a deep fear of ending up there and being a burden."

From this I realised that even though he was in a good place, the thought of what could have been was still too difficult for him to talk about. He had, and still carried, a very real fear of being hospitalised.

She asked whether his mum suffered because it seemed like there were multiple times in a hospital bed and she suffered with it. "Don says, 'After watching Mum, I preferred this way [going suddenly in his sleep] and not that way [slowly fading in a hospital bed].'"

I told Rouna that I knew if Don had an opportunity to choose how he would go; this is what he would have chosen. She said, "Definitely. I'm getting goose bumps all over, which is confirmation for you because it's just not the way he wanted to live his life."

Don went on to say he wanted us (our two children and I) to have a drink together to celebrate his life because this was how he wanted to go. There was extended dialogue between Rouna and Don where he was trying to indicate to Rouna 'the drink', which I think is Baileys, but she was having trouble telling me because she didn't drink. She laughed and said, "He's laughing and telling me I'm hopeless!" That's Don.

He went on to talk about his brother and sisters and his concerns for them. A part of me wondered why he was discussing this until I remembered my instructions to him. I had told him previously that I wanted him to talk to me like he would if he were here because I missed our conversations. Of course, that's what he was doing when talking about family. It's the sort of conversation we would have had. *He was giving me what I had asked for.*

Rouna then said, "I have to tell you, he just feels so great. It's like he passed away and here he is, he's healed, he's with it spiritually and he's physically well."

"Don's saying, 'I'm happy. I feel like freedom. I can go wherever I want. It is freedom.'" Rouna said, "There's no pain and he didn't have to take *anything* with him."

Rouna explained that Don didn't take much negative emotions with him. She said, "Some people I see *it takes them weeks or months because they take so much anger and hatred from this world that they don't heal easily.* There is nothing like that with him. He's a free spirit, he's so good."

Don then said, "I don't want you to hold onto me so that you never ever find anyone else. I feel like you never want to love anyone like you love me, but it's okay to have someone in your life, and I know you are going to say to me no, no, no, but not yet."

The much-anticipated talk with Don

In fact, that was exactly what I was saying. How could he even think I would want to hear this!

Rouna said, "When the time is right you will know and there won't be any guilt from it because you won't be letting go of him. You will go out with friends for dinner and it will be a social situation for you, and you will be happy with that, but he doesn't feel the timing is right for you yet."

I explained, "I had gone out for dinner with a guy I had worked with for years who was offering me a C-level job, but I was so uncomfortable. I was in the restaurant with this guy and the song I associate with Don, 'our' song, played. I hadn't even heard any music in the place before the song started loud and clear."

Rouna asked, "Did you retreat into yourself?" I understood what she meant by this because I was physically there, but mentally I was putting up walls and not engaged in conversation or my surroundings. In a way I zoned out. I probably even shrunk down in my chair. I was trying to disappear. Our reaction when feeling scared is fight, flight or freeze. I froze.

I said, "Yes, I was just wanting to get away. I was putting my toe into the water thinking, can I do this? And I thought, no. It just didn't feel right. I was so uncomfortable."

Then she explained, "When you retreated, Don played the song to bring you back. He was trying to say to you, you are beating yourself up about something that would happen in time, just not now."

I said, "I didn't know what to do. I keep trying things to see what will give me more peace and all that is giving me peace at the moment is being at home and feeling Don is there with me."

"Don says, 'You're doing things like the crossword and journal, that's enough at this stage.'"

Our son's wedding was coming up in a couple of months and Don was telling Rouna there was something about the date. I explained how our son chose May the 4th (be with you) for its *Star Wars* connection. Don wanted me to know our son was getting the support he needed from his partner, and that even though I didn't feel I could support them at the moment, they were being supported.

Don said, "Besides the butterflies, have you seen the bird?"

I said, "First thing in the morning it wakes me up; it's noisy."

He said, "Yes, there's different ways I can connect to you, so don't just focus on the butterflies. Although I didn't prepare you for my death, I gave you enough life skills to get you through this."

This seemed a bit arrogant, but I couldn't complain about the love and life I'd had, so would let that go. He was also pointing out that I hadn't really dealt with a lot of death.

"I know! The only other major one for me was our dog."

Then Don said, "Don't worry about him, he's with me."

It seemed like Don had all the company he needed, and I was the lonely one.

Rouna mentioned Don's sisters, and Don asked me to pass on a message to his younger sister, who he felt was suffering and needed a connection. He said to reinforce, to her, that he didn't suffer and that this was how he wanted to go, and he was concerned she was suffering. Don acknowledged his other sister and brother and said he knew it was a big shock to all of them for him to go.

Rouna then said, "I can't imagine why Don is saying this to me, but it makes him at peace, so I have to say it. He's saying,

'The way I went, the insurance or super ends up better this way.' I'm (Rouna) saying it's not important, and he's saying to him it is. Financially, it's a lot better for Pam and can you imagine the financial burden had I not gone. He says, 'I didn't work hard all my life for the money to go on something I didn't believe in.' To Don, money enables us to enjoy life. To 'waste' it on holding him in a life of misery if he was incapacitated in anyway was unacceptable.

Don is referring to existing not living, and the burden that would be – both financially and emotionally – and this is what he didn't want.

Rouna said, "Don's surprised about the reaction people had (to his death) and the respect they had for him. That was wonderful and he was humbled by it."

I said, "He helped so many people just by being himself. It was just his nature. Time for people and giving was what were important to him."

Rouna said, "I feel his heart is so big. And he was a humble and grounded person. He never showed off when he had money. It was just about being an average bloke, and I really love that about him."

Don changed the subject and Rouna said, "He's saying can you see the difference (I feel he's talking about the reading). Can you see the difference and feel the difference between this and a previous reading, because this is really important for you? Because you need to understand where this connection comes from. He needs you to be able to analyse that and understand that, because if you ever go to anyone else for support (reading) he needs you to be able to feel and just remember that because *'I'm going to be with you all your life. Whatever you are doing in your life, I am always going to be by your side.'*"

I got a sense that this was why I kept having the internal voice saying, *'I can't believe he's left me.'* Annette was telling me he would be there when I called him or in a reading, but Don was reinforcing that he would *always* be beside me. This was the promise he gave me through my soul, and my conscious brain (ego) was trying to make sense of it as it expected to be able to see his presence if he was here.

He said, "While you hear me with the crosswords in your right ear, remember I'm always going to be on your left side. Whenever you are somewhere or walking, I will always be on your left. And you will feel that energy. *The energy is also going to be in the music, it's going to be in things I put in front of you and you will know it's me.*"

Don advised, "The left side is where I want to be because it's the male side, the strength. I'm going to be there at your side, *always* know I'll be there. I'm going to be putting things – not only the butterfly, the birds, the music – there will be things I bring into your life, and don't feel guilty if you don't want to take them. Have a look at them and you make the decision if you want them in your life or not, and that's how I want you to live."

Rouna continued, "And he's saying to you, if someone else comes into your life, 'You don't want it to be like us because you *learned what love is* and you learned because we had the best relationship. And with anyone else it doesn't matter because it's just going to be a relationship. You don't need to learn the lesson about what love is because you have had the best, because we had the best together, it's not me, it's what *we had* that was the best. We could be emotional, we could be spiritual, we could be physical, and the most important thing is that we were *best friends*, and that is really important for him because if we hadn't been best friends, we couldn't have worked together.'"

The much-anticipated talk with Don

I said, "We worked together for twenty-three years, but it was the most amazing adventure that we were lucky enough to call work."

Rouna asked if I'd met my grandmother from my mother's side (Nana Reacie).

"Yes."

I am advised Nana Reacie is around me a lot and that when she is, I am likely to smell a floral scent. Rouna says, "She is finding the strength of the women in the family has not changed, even though times have. She's proud of her daughter, she's proud of you and your daughter and saying, 'Wow! look at them.'"

I'm advised that Archangel Michael is around me. Really giving me strength. Archangel Rafael will come into my life. The different angels will carry me.

Don said, "Don't stop the journal. Write in there whatever you want. Stop it when you want. But don't you dare stop the crosswords!"

"No way will I do that! I won't because it gives me peace because it feels like it's still something we do together."

Rouna then said she felt like one question was unanswered as they – Don and the other spirits – were still there. She asked if I had a question about time or timing.

I choked up, couldn't talk and indicated there were two things.

I was crying but I had to get this question out. I hadn't asked the one big thing I wanted to know, and now Don had prompted me to ask it. It had been eating me up.

I asked, "Why did he die the day before we were going to have a holiday together? I don't understand that. I think it's cruel because he encouraged me to work when in two days, when we would have been going on holiday, we didn't. Why couldn't we have had that holiday together? Why did he encourage me to do all that stuff for work when we could have had that time together?"

Don said, "I didn't want to die *over there*. I didn't want that."

"Does that mean he would have died while we were on holiday?"

Rouna said, "Yes, and he didn't want to travel that way. He didn't want his body brought back on a plane. *The distance was too far*. It's like the only choice he had was to die at home the day before. He didn't want to go that way, away from home and he didn't want to die on his birthday (the day we were going on holiday), and if he had lasted any longer, the only choice he would have had rather than on his birthday was slowly dying in a hospital. That's why he's talking about time."

What could I say to that? This really broke my heart. I could feel the pain in his words (Every time I read this part, while proofing this book, this makes me cry, and I have read it so many times). He really did make the only decision he could. I understood. I said, "I told him so many times since he died that I am so grateful he died in bed beside me."

Rouna said, "He's saying how other people wouldn't understand that. But he felt because of your closeness he knew it would have been more horrible if you had been out of the house and come back, and you wouldn't have known what happened."

"Yes, the way it happened was perfect, for us," I concur.

Rouna asked, "Why is coffee coming into my head?"

"Going for coffee was a thing that was really special for us because it was generally just the two of us, with nothing to

The much-anticipated talk with Don

distract us. We always enjoyed each other's company. I really miss this, every day."

Rouna advised that he was with me all the time and that I was so lucky. "The love you and he have is just amazing."

I said, "I thought I would get a sense of peace from this reading."

Rouna explained, "It's just a process for you at the moment. You do have peace because you know it's him. You needed to go through this and hear all of this."

Don piped in and said, "Isn't it great you didn't have to stop the reading?"

I knew what Don was saying, so I told Rouna, "I was very upset about coming and almost didn't come in."

Rouna confirmed that Don knew that and that he was here and waiting for me. She could see the roses this morning and as soon as she meditated it was yellow roses, and when she started the reading it was the first thing he was going on about. There was no problem whether he was going to come through or not, it was his energy. His calm energy was wonderful.

My second and last question was, "Does he understand the amount of pain that I have?"

Don said, "At least you know that and are acknowledging that pain. If it had been reversed and you went first, the worst thing about it is, I would be terrible because I would be trying to hide that pain, to put on a front. If it was you going, I would be trying to put the kids first and I would be hiding that pain." Rouna continued, "He is so proud that you are not hiding that pain and he's saying don't listen to anyone. It's normal to go through that pain. It's normal to go through that grief. It's okay. It really is. He says, 'I can handle seeing you in pain.' He goes on to say,

'There are going to be situations in the future, treasured moments, grandchildren, but you are also going to feel the loss.'"

Rouna asked me to decide if we were finished. Hah, I could have moved into this woman's house and talked to Don all day, but okay. I had no more questions.

Don said to Rouna, "I'm always there, she knows this. So, you don't have to worry about finishing because I'm always going to be there, not just during a reading. When I'm not there in the physical, whether it's the bird or the butterfly or something else, I'm there in her heart with the music, so she knows I'm always there with her." Rouna said, "So, he's got no problem with us ending."

The session ended. Rouna gave me a CD that I secretly vowed never to listen to. At the time, there was so much grief in me, so much pain, so much to take in, and I misinterpreted some things in my mind. The recording was a blessing because eighteen months later, when I did listen to it, I felt so much love for Don and from Don, his determination to have the reading (which he was early for), and precious statements delivered with pure love. I took comfort in the promise that he would always be at my side and never out of reach, but at this time I was truly suffering unbearable grief. It seemed that not even talking to Don could reduce my suffering at the time.

Talking to Don gave me answers to questions that had been repeatedly on my mind and I had been desperately wanting answers to. Without the psychic's help I would have carried these questions to my deathbed, as so many people do.

Why had he died before our holiday? That was a big one. Did he feel as much grief as I did? And why did I keep saying, "I can't believe you left me?"

I received so many expressions of pure love in this reading, but I do particularly treasure the following:

"He wants you to know he didn't want to leave you, but he had to go."

And his insistence, using words I could see and hear him saying, that I continue with the word game. It was something we both treasured because this particular connection was so strong. We were in sync.

I was also gaining a better understanding of the baggage and healing required if we hold hatred and anger in our last breath. By the end, Don was mostly love and fun and kindness. Because of this and because he was an old soul, he went through the healing quickly and he was able to make contact more quickly and clearly than was anticipated.

This is the most beautiful ending he could have given me because he was adamantly reassuring me of his continued presence beside me.

I look at Don's photos and I see the person he was 'then', and over thirty-seven years there were many variations of the man I love deeply. Now I have a sense of Don that is not a feeling tied to a specific photo, but a vivid and intense feeling kept in my heart.

I don't know whether that makes sense to others, but the now Don, who I interact with through readings and messages, is not the Don who died beside me. This is Don radiating pure love and support that is focused directly to me. I am blessed and I know it!

I also get a sense that how he phrased 'dying over there', 'the distance was too far' and 'not wanting his body brought back in a plane', links how he orchestrated this death (avoiding those three points) with the death he experienced in his most recent previous life. Details of this he shared in a later reading, which we will get to in Chapter 25.

from my heart to yours . . .

In a way I felt this reading was too soon for me. I was grateful to have the recording so that I could understand everything I had missed because I was too consumed by grief to comprehend most of it at the time. But in reality, if it had been too soon, it would not have happened on that day.

If you choose to connect through a medium and you experience delays, know that it is intentional. It will happen at the right time for you and them. Timing may also be based on connecting you to the right psychic/reader.

Don also took this opportunity in the reading to talk to me about the prior tarot reading. I had felt strongly that I didn't want her to connect me with Don, and unbeknownst to me, he had also stopped her from connecting with him.

Don says it was as if the tarot reader was reading out of a book, no compassion, and he doesn't want me to believe that is the sort of connection I would have with him, because it's supposed to come from the heart, a soul connection.'

This is what I was saying in Chapter 11 – the frequency this communication travels along *has* to be love.

This was incredibly beautiful for me to hear. We both said no to communicating through the tarot reader. Did he really die? I thought, because this is what we did in life, we were in sync, we were both looking out for each other to protect the love/soul connection we had. We were on different planes but still focused on protecting the other.

In each interaction I'm looking for how much of 'my Don' remains and his statement, "I can handle seeing you in pain." jarred with me because this does not sound like 'my Don'. He was crying at the start of the reading so although he says he can handle seeing me in pain, he's not unaffected by it. In life he would never have said these words without trying to fix it. But the circumstances have changed, and he can see clearly the outcome, the end of the pain, the reason I chose to experience this. He sees what I can't. My soul's purpose in having this experience.

This reading was a blessing. Don was at the session with Rouna even before it was due to start. He wasn't just keen to communicate with me, he was mentally and emotionally ready. More ready than I was. This experience was about both of us and what would be right for us. I heard what I needed to hear at this time.

Months later, I met a woman whose husband had 'died' suddenly, although he lingered for weeks in a coma. After he passed, she wanted to communicate with him and was interested in my story, but what unfolded for her was completely different.

In her reading she was told her husband was a young soul and was struggling to come to terms with his own death. He was not yet able to communicate directly with her as Don had with me. She desperately wanted the communication, and although there had been communication with him through the medium, she felt this was not enough. I have felt that, too, even with everything I received. It will never be the same as having them here, but you need to find comfort in knowing you are still connected. This woman planned to wait a couple more months and try again.

I also recommend recording the session. I didn't understand or appreciate most of what was said until I listened again well after the reading. That's when I heard the precious expressions of love that I pull out periodically for a mood boost. I love Don saying, "And don't you dare give up the word game." At the time it was just words with Don's humour, then I saw it for what it was. His need matched my need to have this deep, continued connection, even if it was just in a game. I still play the game every night.

In this reading Don also mentioned our daughter was looking after others. It took two years before she admitted she hadn't really grieved. She thought she was just better at coping with death because she'd had more firsthand experience with it than I had. In reality, she had avoided coping with it by focusing on others, including me. This is also what Don said he would have done. The apple doesn't fall far from the tree!

Regardless, I didn't want or need this extra attention. Although I appreciated her being there for me, what she did wasn't really about me or for me. It was how *she* coped, by pushing it down and not allowing herself the time to grieve.

Be aware of people managing their grief through yours. There is no short cut or 'way around' for anyone. She ended up grieving, but much later. And it wasn't a mistake that she experienced grief later; her grieving came when she had the right support person in her life.

And finally, I could have carried baggage for years on why Don went when he did. Instead, I asked him to please help me understand.

So, Don patiently explained what decisions he was able to make and the limited options he had within a specific timeframe to go 'on his terms'. And most importantly, he stressed that he didn't want to leave me, but he had no choice. These all gave me a sense of closure and some peace. This was important in my healing and grief management because I had made his *death* about me. "How could you do this to me?"

So, whether it's a recent passing or someone who has been gone for a long time, it's up to you to find peace and if its answers you feel you need, you now know, all you have to do is ask them. It's never too late.

I don't like to say
you broke my heart
because that suggests
you don't love me anymore,
but I know you broke me.
When I started putting
all the pieces together,
I found there was
a big part missing.
You weren't just my partner,
you were a part of me.

Pam Eade
From my journal

16

I'm looking for peace but only finding pieces

6th April – four months, two days since Don left this world

Feelings of hopelessness plagued me after the reading with Rouna, and I was getting angry. It was at this point I contemplated taking too many sleeping pills. I had been prescribed them but had never taken any. I got them out, put them on the bedside table and said, "I am ready!" I went downstairs to get water (more of a delaying tactic, I think). When I turned the kitchen lights on, they were flashing like crazy. Don was making sure I knew he was there with me. I didn't take the pills, but you probably guessed that because the story didn't end there.

My main problem was I couldn't contemplate a future without pain, so the next day I wrote out some goals where I could see my future differently. International travel, an apartment overlooking water, financial independence, a puppy, a satisfying career and a degree (maybe).

I don't know what I expected but felt I had worked out that I needed to put something positive in my future. The idea of a holiday without Don was abhorrent, but at the same time I knew I needed *a* break, or *I* would break.

Within a few days I was so angry and started ranting to him how unfair this was. I hated the person I'd become. I'd never been an angry person. Fortunately, my rants were out loud, and I could hear the absurdity of what I was saying. This was totally out of control. I recognised that I was placing myself in a victim state. I made my first rule, appropriately named #1, and the only rule I made:

#1 Do not act like a victim if you do not want to be one.

Although Don was not there physically, I knew he was there and therefore a witness to my angry outbursts. I felt ashamed. I felt stuck in a nightmare. I was not better, I was worse.

The shock had definitely fully worn off, and reality was a bitch. The anger carried on for days. It was exhausting. I knew it was a stage of grief but what was the point of reading about something when you already had a front-row seat to your own drama. I was powerless to stop the outbursts. It seemed another injustice in this grieving process was to become a person I didn't recognise or like.

All I wanted was to feel at peace. Every other desire could come after that. I was still doing as much as possible each day from my self-care survival toolkit (see Part III). It was in my head at this stage, but when I wanted to change my state of mind, I mentally went through what I knew would help me and decided which ones to do. I needed a better filing system.

I felt that if I did something completely different it would give my mind a break. Prior to Don's death, we were discussing renovations, so I wanted to do something that would consume my attention. In less than 4 weeks, family would be in our home for Harley's wedding.

I decided to put my energy into building the fire pit that we had planned. There was a lot of really heavy work which involved digging up large stones that had formed a low retaining wall, but I was determined to complete what we had planned to do. Stacey helped me.

Then 12 months later, to get myself out of a mental rut I did the same. We had a 'dog-leg' path that I wanted curved and joined to the fire pit; without thinking, I picked up a brick from the path and stacked it around the corner. Before I knew it, I had moved all the bricks and stacked them, as a bricklayer would.

I felt Don's presence. I did things without hesitation. I knew he was channelling his can-do anything handyman persona into me. I created the outline for the curved path, spent days packing down the crusher dust and then laid the bricks back down in a lovely arrangement. The path I created with Stacey's help was perfect. I know it was done with Don's help. Most importantly though, both projects consumed me and diverted my thoughts from grieving for a while. It gave me time with the me that had been buried under so much grief. I felt alive.

There was also a period where I removed Don's photos for a few days because it was just too distressing to see his face. I would not have thought to do that, but a friend whose father was struggling after losing his wife had removed photos when they were upsetting. It worked for me too. Then I put them all back when I was calmer.

I found a guided meditation that talked me through meeting up with Don in a room in my head (refer YouTube: 'Coping with Grief' by Jason Stephenson). This was a meditation I did once I'd gone to bed and finished my journal entry. The meditation allowed me to do what had become impossible. I walked into his arms; I held his hand and I sat beside him with my cheek on his chest. We talked! All the things I missed I brought into the meditation, like having a coffee together. It asks you to create a room for your loved one to visit you in.

A couple of times I visualised our room, but it wasn't easy to hold on to. The room in my mind was light and looked out to a balcony, which looked over a body of water. This image became my default, and it felt right because it was easy to hold the view. This meditation worked for me as it gave me a sense of peace when it finished, as if I *had* connected with Don. I have always said that with Don, from the moment we met, I felt a calmness in his presence. This was what I had after the meditation. I also found I was sleeping better and my state of mind when I woke was calmer.

Don was a wonderful and flawed human being and was now a wonderful and pure spirit. The love and support he gave me from the other side were reminiscent of the love and support I had before. He was the most attentive husband and my best friend. Impossible as it seemed, my love for Don had grown as it was no longer seen through a haze of earthly issues, money, job, physical ailments, ageing and uncertainty. Now there was only pure love.

I was open to how messages were sent from where Don was, so when a dragonfly came into the house, I managed to catch it and put it outside, then googled whether there was any message or symbolism in this.

'Dragonflies symbolise a change in self-realisation, mental and emotional maturity and understanding the deeper meaning of life. The dragonfly exemplifies living in the moment and living life to the fullest. By living in the moment, you are aware of who you are, where you are, what you are doing, what you want, what you don't want.' Yes. This was a 're-evaluation of self' process. Thank you for the message.

Now that I understood why I heard certain lyrics, I didn't doubt whether a song was from Don. If it was, I *felt his energy in the music*, as he said I would. That was what made it louder and clearer to me. Most of the time I could understand the relevance of the lyrics or song; however, there was a song that caused me to pause every time it came on as I felt it was a message, but I couldn't understand the significance of the lyrics. *'What do the lyrics 'I'm coming home' by Shepherd mean?'* I wondered. I was sure I would understand the message in due course.

I was told recently that grief is exhausting. I hadn't looked at it that way. It most definitely is!

When I got really low, I watched comedy on YouTube until I had watched enough to fully embed a new mindset. I felt more in control of my emotional state after that.

I also had a reminder that life is about living. My life, since Don died, had been about death. Not just for Don but for the part of me that died as well. Yet life is about growth. If it doesn't grow in some way, it shrivels up and dies. I had to do something.

I wished I wasn't carrying so much sadness with me when it was our son Harley's wedding, but the sense of doing it on my own was always in my head. Don's seat beside me at the wedding was empty, but I had brought his long leather coat and hung it over the chair. There were lots of family and friends around and the wedding was so much fun and a joyous occasion, filled with laughter. Don would have loved it! So, the absolute hardest part was seeing Don's photo on a memorial wall at the wedding. Everything about my grieving up to that point had felt deeply personal. This was a public confirmation he was gone. I couldn't bear to look at it but was conscious of his face in my peripheral vision the whole time.

During the speeches, the lights at the end of the room over the memorial table started to flicker. Spiritually aware people knew it was someone sending a message. I was trying to get my daughter's attention so she would see it, but someone, probably not so spiritually aware, decided they had to turn the 'faulty' lights off. I can confirm it wasn't Don flicking the lights, although I didn't find out until a few days later. A member of my daughter-in-law's family had discovered in a reading it was a deceased aunt who had flicked them because she was annoyed people were talking during Nicole's grandad's speech.

This was a time with a lot of family and friends around and it was upsetting that Don went before so many people who were/are sicker than he ever was. Not that I wished them any ill will, just a longer life for Don. What I missed the most was sharing.

We had been together so long; we had our own roles in everything that happened. Don and I were yin and yang. We would go to something like this wedding and he could talk to anyone and everyone, so I didn't need to. I would throw in some comments, but he carried the conversations with humour and intellect. Now I had to talk because he wasn't saying anything. So, I was reminded in everything that his part in our relationship and shared experiences was now empty. I still felt I needed to acknowledge that Don was with me, he was sharing these experiences, although I still felt alone.

It had been almost six months and I asked myself where I was through the grieving process. Halfway, almost there or still a long way to go?

I could also see I was in cycles of good periods and not-so-good periods, and that if I just hung in there, I would get through the bad cycle and into another good one.

I look back on this period in my journal when he had been gone twenty months and marvel at how naïve I was. My poor eyes, to have had to channel so many tears. I wonder why I still put makeup on every morning. In an attempt to channel 'normal', I suppose.

Sometimes it felt like nothing was changing, but in fact I was like a chrysalis, I was being rebuilt, restructured, and all the pieces would fall into place and make me whole. I would emerge feeling like a complete person again. One day.

from my heart to yours...

I believe part of what makes life difficult is that life goes on and normal things continue to happen. It's the presence of normal that makes it harder. If everything was different it would be more 'acceptable'. Makes sense, right?

I don't always know why I'm emotional but have decided it just doesn't matter why. I have come to the realisation that grief and loss are an unavoidable but, by default, acceptable cost of living.

I highly recommend the YouTube meditation 'Coping with Grief' by Jason Stephenson. It was something that brought me closer to Don (other than the nightly word game). At first, I thought it was my imagination creating his presence, but the more I learned about life and death, the more I appreciated why he seemed so real. I had opened a space, where the vibration that is in everything put us on the same frequency where we did, in fact, connect.

At our son's wedding the salute to past family on the memorial table was a beautiful tribute, acknowledging their continued presence and an impact on family that was still felt. I love that the lights were flickered by the in-law's family. It shows their continued presence in all of our lives, especially for celebrations.

It helps to look back as it is only in this that you will truly be able to see how far you have come.

Past family members were acknowledged on the memorial table and specifically for me, Don's watch on my arm and his coat on my chair.

Piglet: How do you spell love?
Pooh: You don't spell it.
You feel it.

Winnie the Pooh
A.A. Milne

17
Love knows no boundaries

26th May – five months, twenty-two days since Don left this world

I couldn't conjure up an image of Don in my head. I could see him as he looked in specific photos in my head, but I couldn't create an image. This caused little panic attacks until I decided I would not allow it to do so.

I realised I needed to stop focusing on the Don that was and content myself with the presence he had now. I suffered more when I thought of Don as a physical being when, in reality, the emotional connection was a stronger bond, and I didn't need him there to feel that.

With the absence of the physical, the emotional was heightened. The same as when your hearing is more acute if you close your eyes and focus on listening.

Don still flashed the lights and sent butterflies and feathers every day. Most days there were songs that stood out. I knew he put his energy into Cher's 'If I could turn back time' and Meatloaf's 'I would do anything for love'. He loved those two songs and artists and probably welcomed this superpower so that he could play them at will.

He also put his energy into REO Speedwagon's 'I'm going to keep on loving you'. One time after I'd said, 'I don't want to keep doing this' (living equals suffering), the lyrics he energised/amplified on the radio were about not giving up and that it wasn't in my blood to be a quitter.

Even when I felt calm, I still carried tightness in my chest. I went back to Andy to get the 'stuck' emotion lifted. My eyes still leaked while I had the treatment as I was there mainly because the emotion was so close to the surface.

Andy said I was a spiritual sleeper, and I was waking up. Okay. He saw a lion, which symbolised (my) strength. Yes, a good token for me, I love cats!

Andy asked whether I was sleeping well, and I explained I was waking during the night. This was something that had happened since Don died. When asked whether I woke at the same time each night, I said yes, about 4am. He advised I was waking at this time because my soul still held the trauma of being woken when Don physically died, which was at 4am. I hadn't even realised the significance of this.

He said he saw me giving a speech on stage to a lot of people. I have been told this before but have discounted it because if you knew me, you would understand how unlikely this is. But I also never thought I would write a book so who knows what is in my future! I thought Don would always be here, physically, so obviously it's not going to be as I expect.

Partway through the session, I felt this incredible calmness that developed into a feeling of intense positive energy (it's hard to explain). I had no idea what was happening, except that it reminded me of sinking into a warm, relaxing bath or the feeling I generated when I was away for work and I thought of Don. Like a wave of love, but this felt like it lasted much longer, although I had no concept of time and felt suspended in this warm serene emotion.

I was calm and felt like I was floating, so I was surprised when Andy spoke to me. The session had finished. He said, "You had a visitor." Understandably, if Andy was working with my energy he would be as aware of an energy surge in my body as I was. That made sense. I relegated this to the back of my mind because I hadn't fully grasped what had happened or what his words meant. But his choice of words was interesting. I knew what I felt and was convinced it was Don but this was massive and with a new experience it was natural to want some validation.

I had an 'ah ha' moment about twelve months later. I went to a meditation with Sufian Chaudhary, who described how his body was flooded with unconditional love when he met Archangel Uriel (I know how this sounds), but the strange thing was, it was someone else putting exactly what I had felt into words.

The pure love energy surge was the most incredible experience. I wondered whether Andy told Don he couldn't kiss my forehead again. But now I knew Don could do this, I looked forward to my next session with Andy. I knew how blessed I was. I had another priceless memory.

So, I told myself it didn't matter that I couldn't bring his image into my head; I had photos for that. Having any other view would not be supporting my wellbeing.

I continue to have a sense of Don as he is now. He's not clearly defined but he's smiling at me and I can feel the love radiating out of his smile. He wants me to be happy. This is the Don, in my mind's eye, that is with me no matter where I am.

When Don was fifty, I didn't mourn the loss of forty-year-old Don. Now, although physical Don has gone, I have a sense of current Don that is not based on physical but on feeling. And the feeling is strong.

from my heart to yours...

Everything happens for a reason; it just sometimes takes a while to understand what that something means.

Hindsight, the illegitimate child of wisdom, later allows you to see things in a different perspective. I think writing this book has allowed me to reflect more often than I normally would on life. I believe I am now more attuned to seeing wrinkles in life and either search my mind for an answer or say to myself, what this is will be revealed when and if I need to understand. So much of what I have experienced I could not have predicted. It has been a sci-fi soap opera with undertones of a tragic comedy.

I think one of the most beautiful lessons I have learned is that the physical is not where life really is. It's in the vibration. Everything is energy vibrating, and love is the ultimate vibration. It's not about physical location. You can feel a deep, tingling love vibration for someone in the next room, across town, in another country and, most definitely, those not in this world. I take a lot of satisfaction in sitting quietly, imagining Don smiling at me and just feeling the love bloom inside me.

Don't discount anything that happens to you, especially if it comes with a surge of feeling. You are still connected. You are still loved.

These mountains you are carrying, you were only supposed to climb.

Najwa Zebian

18

"I understand"

5th June – six months, one day since Don left this world

I felt like a hamster on a wheel. I was working hard but the scenery wasn't changing.

I had previously used psychic readings as a way of getting clarity when I felt stuck, so I booked a session with Melanie, our psychic friend, and, of course, Don.

At this time, I also had a problem with a rat that had started sitting outside my office window at home munching on berries. I have always had an irrational fear of rats and mice. I named the rat Steve. Why? Because it was a non-threatening name and I have a long-held habit and coping mechanism of naming things to change my perspective of them.

Back to Steve. My husband had gone, and I lived alone with Winnie, a cat that didn't understand that his job was not that of a sloth! I'd named my previous cat Kilmousky so she would know her purpose, but she didn't. My husband and son had always protected me from rodents but neither of them was there.

The reading would help me focus on other things. Melanie told me I wasn't selling the house yet and to just look at doing maintenance. This was good. It was something for me to focus on.

I casually mentioned the appearance of (rat-faced) Steve, and Melanie advised he had come into my life because this was a period for me to let go of fears. Steve would not hurt me; he meant me no harm. Two days later, I ran outside to shoo crows away that were eyeing Steve as dinner while he was focused on enjoying his berries. I came back inside and saw that Winnie had now seen Steve and was 'interested'. I ran outside again and brought Winnie in. This was so out of character for me, but I felt if Steve meant me no harm, and he was there to help me, then I could ensure no harm came to him. He never returned, and my irrational fear of rats is now more rational, so his job was done.

In the session with Annette in December 2017, she mentioned that the soul of the baby we had lost was with Don in the reading. Don was sixty-three when we found out I was pregnant, and the pressure of me becoming the main earner had started. I had gone to the doctor because I was so emotional and wasn't coping. We were shifting house and I was starting a new role in management with a new company. Instead of giving me something for stress she told me I was pregnant! Had we not terminated that pregnancy, this little soul would have been a ten-year-old at the time Don died.

Melanie went on to say that this sweet little soul was with Don right now and that she would come into the family as a grandchild. And a blessing (Stacey had been trying to get pregnant for so long. Maybe her time was coming).

She asked if I had seen Don (in spirit) yet, which I hadn't. She said he would appear when I had a clear perspective and less grief blocking me.

"I understand"

Don said, through Melanie, that *'he would never leave me'*. He was showing her that he was sweeping the path in front of me, making sure all opportunities were ready when I was. This was what he was doing for me and was a wonderful illustration of the man he was in life.

Melanie said, "Don wants you to know he's gone home." (me: OMG!) Then Don went on to reiterate that this is where he is, through Melanie of course. I was sitting there speechless.

The significance of this to me was mind-blowing. I had felt his energy in the lyrics about coming home ('Coming home' by Sheppard) and he played it with his energy so often. I knew it was a message and I would eventually understand what he was telling me. He wasn't coming home, *to me*, I knew that. But now I understood. HE went home! This was the biggest comfort to me. Even in life, when you are separated, it is a comfort to know the other is 'at home', and the wonderful thing was that although Don was home, he was still with me. He didn't feel further away; he felt closer because I knew where he was.

He was at home and would be there when it was my turn to go (home). Seeing death from this perspective feels so right. 'Home' is an emotive word and means so much. It is where our family is. It's a safe place (for most). This is every person's version of Heaven. Through religions, Heaven denotes exclusivity and denied access for some. *But everyone gets to go HOME when they die.* This is clarity that we all need, and we couldn't get a better destination. *This message was a gift from Don.*

Melanie said, "I don't know what this means, but Don's asking, 'How's the washing machine?' I have no idea why he would ask that."

My first reaction was that it was strange he would ask about the one appliance that was no longer a problem. The oven was limping to retirement and only worked on one setting. The dishwasher drawer had to be held a certain way to open it. The fridge was ancient. The air-conditioning remotes couldn't be replaced; it was too old. The washing machine was the newest appliance we had.

Why was I confused? Because I had made the mistake of thinking Don was now someone else, but when I heard the words said by the Don I had lived with, I saw his sense of humour and understood the message. Our conversations used to be entertaining, never boring, because we both had a great sense of humour. I never had trouble interpreting his train of thought before when he'd say something cryptic but cheeky, and that's when I realised.

Don was using humour to acknowledge a painful period in my life. As mentioned earlier, in an outburst of anger, I had kicked and sworn at the washing machine and told Don to get his butt back here to fix the bloody thing.

I had assumed because I was alone that no-one had witnessed my outburst, which was good because I was ashamed of how out of control I was. I had also never told anyone about this. No witnesses, except Don, because he was with me always. The over-the-top burst of anger was so out of character for me, which is one of the reasons he'd mentioned it, with humour. He was reaffirming, subtly, that he understood, and that I needed to know I was not alone; he was with me even in my darkest hours.

Don was now telling me that Ralph was there with him as well and reminded me that Ralph would come back when I was ready. Ralph was our beloved Border Collie and was the dog I identified as my previous most devastating experience of loss. I had been told he would come back, but my expectation was that I would be *led* to the right puppy. The last person I could trust to read the signs during my grief was me. I was scared. Was it possible for me to pick the wrong puppy? It's not like I could rely on the puppy. All puppies look at you as if to say, 'I'm the one you're looking for.'

Melanie said she could see his little face. He was small and light coloured. I asked how I would know him, and she said just look into his eyes. I then asked Don to name the puppy. Melanie said, "He said Sparky," and that was it; I would start looking for Sparky.

Don also took this opportunity to recommend books that he felt would be helpful for me to understand where he was. These books were about the other side of life, aka life after death.

You can't get any higher recommendation than to have a book on the 'other side' endorsed from the other side.

The books were:

Life on the Other Side by Sylvia Browne

Journey of Souls by Michael Newton

Talking to Heaven by James van Praagh

I read *Life on the Other Side* first. When referencing where Don is, I prefer to call it 'home' (after this reading) but that would be confusing in this book, so throughout I refer to 'home' as the 'other side'. I found this book enlightening.

I was sure I had read *Talking to Heaven* before but because it was published a while ago, I couldn't get it electronically so I delayed looking at that one.

I had *Journey of Souls* already as an electronic book. It is a series of case studies from Michael Newton's research, which gives it a balanced feel and speaks to my analytical brain.

Although I had read this book before, I only remembered one specific case in the book. A woman had a pain in her temple that doctors couldn't find a cause for. In a past-life regression it was discovered she had shot herself in the head in this exact spot in her previous life. I figured I would read it again later when I felt compelled to.

Not long after this I was at a café, and for some reason my coffee order was forgotten, so I had more uninterrupted time available than usual. I started reading *Journey of Souls*. I got to an interview and I knew immediately this was *a message from Don*. All difficult episodes in our life – from catastrophic to annoying – we had shared, but his death was something where I felt I was suffering alone.

I think we all have an expectation that no suffering exists on the other side, whereas my suffering here on Earth was off the charts. Yet, I knew Don had cried in the first couple of readings. In *Journey of Souls*, the person – under hypnosis – is dying in her husband's arms, and although she expresses freedom from the body, she is reluctant to leave her husband. She said she was wanting her husband to feel the deep love she had for him and wanted him to know she was okay and that they would be together again. I felt so strongly that Don was saying, *'I wanted you to read this because this is what I was feeling for you when I died. I didn't want to leave you knowing the suffering this would cause you, but I had no choice.'*

While I was reading this part in the book, 'I did it my way' started playing in the café. This song epitomised Don, which was why it was one of his funeral songs. He was acknowledging that this was the message he wanted me to receive.

During my multiple edits of this book, every time I read the italicised words above; they made me cry. Don obviously channelled these words to me; they were *his* words, they had his energy in them, so I felt it was an absolute truth and felt the raw emotion in them. I understood.

In fact, I understood so much more every time I got to speak with Don. So much of my healing was coming from him. He knew what would provide me comfort, he knew how my mind worked, the information he gave me was on-point and perfectly timed. I really could not imagine doing this without him.

In addition to granddad Ernest, Don also had the soul of the baby we didn't have and Ralph with him in readings. The significance of their presence was revealed to me. What a gift to know they were coming to join me here.

Our children have lives and homes of their own. I was essentially on my own (sorry Winnie, but admit it, you're a part-time companion). Now, both the baby soul and Ralph/Sparky were coming back and would be in my life as blessings and to help ease my pain and loneliness. Of course, neither of them was there yet and I didn't have any idea on timing.

from my heart to yours . . .

Don advised he went HOME to give me comfort and so I could share this information with you in this book. Regardless of whether you are wondering where your loved one is, or concerned about what happens when you die, I hope you can find comfort in Don's advice that he is experiencing an elated sense of freedom and is free from pain and fear, and he is home.

He reunited with passed loves ones and also never left the loved ones still here. I know this because he met up with and introduced Ernest, his grandad; he let us know he met up with Stacey's friend Amanda; and when Stacey made a positive, life-changing decision, he was there, in a reading, with his mum and they were toasting Stacey with red wine. And, of course, his continued presence in my life, as I have documented many times in my story.

Don was at home with our soul family and passed family and friends *and* he was still here. Really, what is there to be worried about with death? The worst part of death, I think, is not dying but living with grief; an experience that is bittersweet because it only exists because of deep love.

We are all going home. This is good news for everyone still walking this Earth.

When the winds of change blows, some people build walls and others build windmills.

Chinese Proverb

19
Stick didn't work? Put carrots in the future

14th July – seven months, ten days since Don left this world

I had been beating myself up for so long. That technique was not working. I couldn't bully myself into being 'better'. So, I put two carrots in my future.

The carrots were events intended to change things significantly. They were deliberately planned to ignite something in my life. Like jumper starts are to a dead engine. I was looking for 'joy'. Ironically, it's my middle name, but I wasn't finding it within me, so I had to look elsewhere.

Life with Don had always been stimulating, exciting and every day held fun. I came to realise that if I didn't create fun in my life it would just be blah. Don had always been naturally courageous and adventurous. I needed to do something BIG! I wanted to be courageous!

I needed a holiday, but one I wouldn't have done with Don otherwise it would just remind me of his absence. As animals can raise my spirits more than anything else, I looked for a volunteer program with orangutans but found elephants instead.

Don and I loved elephants. Tick. It was in Thailand and we had been there before. Tick. Thailand holidays were affordable. Tick. It just felt right. Tick.

I hesitated several times during the interview, confirmation and deposit-paying process. I go a lot on what feels right, and it just felt wrong organising a holiday, especially a wow one, without Don. But the feeling of wrongness was a tinge of guilt for creating something good purely because of Don's death. It was, however, essential for me to prove to myself I could have an interesting life. He would be with me in spirit anyway, so I chose a holiday I knew he would have enjoyed me doing.

I was determined to be on this holiday for what would have been our 36th wedding anniversary. This annual celebration was more important to us than birthdays, and I didn't want to be on my own on that day, so the trip was booked for the end of October. I knew on a deep level that I had to do this. I felt propelled to go, so I signed up as a volunteer at the Elephant Nature Park in Chiang Mai – wow!

The first week would be at the park; the second, in the jungle. I didn't even like camping, so this was a major step for me, designed to give me some purpose and bring joy into my life. It would be huge with regards to my personal growth, which felt like it had been stunted for just over seven months.

The other carrot in my future was to find the puppy. This story started before Don died.

While we are wandering through life, our path ahead is being prepared. I had no concept of this earlier in my life, but the older I get, the more I see this. I have no doubt about it now, but sometimes, when life is just a series of challenges, you start to question the fairness and purpose of life. *'Why is this happening?'*

When Don died, I felt I had no control over my life, and from thereon I had absolutely no faith in my future; but some magnetic force had brought us together thirty-seven years earlier, and, as a result of that unexpected meeting, I got more from life than I ever could have imagined. I was getting ready for life to give me that next big leap into whatever was going to make life worth living again. The key is to be open and trust that good things are coming. Easier said than done. I decided I would just keep moving until things clicked.

Nine months before Don died, we were in Nimbin on a whim. We didn't know anything about the place and found ourselves in a rural hippy town. We rarely took off to an unknown place on the spur of the moment, but a friend mentioned a bed and breakfast and a swimming pool in the rocks that was filled by the sea's waves. It sounded wonderful and we needed to get away, relax and think. This was a breadcrumb on my life path.

A trip that should have been two hours took over four hours as we got lost while using GPS (I know, right), so we ended up stopping for afternoon tea in a little town. A Border Collie puppy was at the café and the desire to get one (again) was incredibly strong. A seed was planted that opened our minds; we were seriously considering getting a puppy.

We had 'run away' for the weekend because work stress levels were turning into panic attacks, so while in Nimbin we stopped at a tarot reader who was set up on the sidewalk. During the reading, she told me there was a dog on the other side that had come forward. I've had other readings that Ralph had appeared in. He was the much-loved Border Collie we had between 1993 and 2005. This was the first time he had a message for me. The tarot reader said that he wanted me to know that he was ready to come back when I needed him. Wow!

Don's initial reaction was, "Let's start looking for a puppy." But after some discussion, we decided to hold off until we knew the time was right. Being randomly reminded of Ralph twice on a random trip ensured there was going to be a puppy in the future.

It wasn't until Don died that I realised why Ralph had sent me the message. Don's death ripped my life apart and I didn't have anything to hold me together. I was going to need Ralph to help me through unimaginable loneliness. I hadn't experienced loneliness since Don had come into my life when I was eighteen.

So, *Higher Power et al.* already had a plan for me before I even knew I needed one. It prepares you while things are being put in place. Everything happens for a reason, but quite often we can't see the perfect synchronicity of events without hindsight.

In 1993 I decided I wanted to get a dog. Ten years earlier I'd had a Newfoundland, but I needed to downsize this time. I researched breeds and chose a Border Collie – medium-sized dog with a seventeen-year life expectancy and the highest canine IQ.

I found a litter of puppies and took Don on a long trip to see them. From the litter of seemingly identical puppies I chose one. He fell asleep in my arms and I fell in love with him. Don wasn't so easily convinced and said we should 'think about it' (which meant his fifty percent of the decision was a 'no'). I covertly asked the breeder to hold onto him as I had something coming up that I felt would change Don's mind. A birthday party!

The night before Don's birthday we went to what he thought was a colleague's business Christmas party. Instead, it was a 'this is your life' surprise fiftieth party for him.

Over one hundred friends and family attended, including people from Australia, Don's English and Math teacher from high school and his high-school girlfriend. Preparation had started five months earlier and the effort that had gone into creating this special event was obvious. Don wasn't just surprised; he was stunned.

At the end of the 'this is your life' production, our dear friend and compere, Guy Cater (also the MC at Don's funeral and both Stacey and Harley's weddings), asked Don in front of the audience, "Now, Don, doesn't Pam deserve that dog?" Without hesitation, Don willingly and enthusiastically said, "Yes!"

Ralph was our hairy-legged son and grew up with our children. Don named him Ralph so he would be the only dog who could say his own name.

The next day we made the long trip to pick him up. Ralph was a special dog. Incredibly loved. Don never regretted this decision. Ralph migrated from New Zealand to Australia with us in 1995 and again in 2005. He died at thirteen human years with cancer in the jaw, and we had to have him put to sleep.

I carried an enormous amount of guilt from having ended his life, even though it was the humane thing to do. For the next ten years, whenever we spoke his name or saw a Border Collie, regret and tears would flow. The 'chance' meeting of a Border Collie puppy when we got lost on the way to Nimbin was special. There were no tears, only joy.

So, Ralph was the dog who had appeared in readings and then gave me the message he would come back to me when I was ready.

We had often talked about Ralph and, on one occasion, when telling a friend about the reading and Ralph coming back, he advised us that dogs don't have souls. It was an insensitive thing to say and I don't know that he was speaking as a Buddhist or was just a jerk.

I have never accepted beliefs that don't resonate with my heart and it doesn't matter how old a religion is. Even Buddha is quoted as saying, *"Believe nothing, no matter where you read it or who has said it, not even if I have said it, unless it agrees with your own reason and your own common sense."*

It is my view that outside of God (*Higher Power et al.*) is love, everything else is man-made. *Higher Power et al.* only trades in love. I chose to believe Ralph's soul came into my readings because we were attached by love. If you have ever wondered whether your pets have a soul, my answer to you is YES!

Throughout life, we meet people and animals we have a deeper connection to. I have no doubt that connection is deepest when it is at soul level. Don and I had that connection. Ralph and I had that connection. I knew in my heart Ralph was coming back and I now understood why.

Naturally, I was worried about *finding* Ralph, and I wasn't expecting him to come back as a Border Collie. I knew he would be a small dog but didn't know what to look for. And, coming back when I was ready wasn't anywhere close to specific.

As mentioned in the previous chapter, a reading with Melanie had reiterated that Ralph would come back, and the expectation was soon. I now knew he would be small and light coloured.

At this point in my grief I did nothing proactively. I waited for things to happen that I would then respond to. I did, however, google 'where is Sparky', in the hope I would find him that way. It wasn't going to be that easy! I did know I couldn't afford anything expensive so figured I would find him in a rehoming situation. I also checked the animal adoption organisations.

Stacey was also keen to get a puppy into 'our' lives. She found a little Jack Russell on the web that was being rehomed and I liked him, so she called. He was still available because someone hadn't come back for him that afternoon. But before we could make the hour-long trip, we were advised he had gone. Okay, so not Sparky.

Three weeks after I had spoken to Melanie, I still wasn't sure how to find him. The little Jack Russell I missed out on did, however, give me a sense that this was the breed I was looking for. Stacey and I were at a shopping centre one Saturday and found Jack Russell puppies in a pet shop. One was left. He was cute. I held him; he wouldn't look me in the eye, and he wriggled all the time. I knew I couldn't go home with that puppy.

I decided to get my nails done in an effort to feel happier, and Stacey spent her time looking for 'Sparky' on the internet. She found a small Jack Russell/Maltese cross litter at a home about forty-five minutes away. I looked at photos and said, "I'm only interested in one of them." Again, a person was going to be choosing one before we got there, so if it was meant to be...

We left straight away, and on the way there I was nervous and talked to Don in my head. I asked him to please give me a sign if this was the right one.

During the drive I told Stacey that when I had picked Ralph out of the litter, we'd had this connection and he'd fallen asleep in my arms. Stacey said, "Well, they are puppies so you can't expect that to happen again."

We pulled up outside the complex and, as we were walking towards the drive, a butterfly flew across our path. Classic Don. We took it as a good sign, but I was still nervous.

Part of my doubt was also because of the cost. If this was Sparky, why was I being sent to a puppy that was going to cost me more money than I had?

I watched the puppies playing with Stacey, and knew he was the one. I picked him up and looked into his eyes just before he went to sleep in my arms! Unbelievable. The whole hour we were there, I just held him while he slept, and the other puppies played. While I sat on the couch with him in my arms, I sobbed, unable to talk. My daughter made small talk with the lady selling the puppies. Awkward!

I know the feeling of grief and this feeling was a close relative. While I cried, this incredibly powerful and physical emotion was pushing up in my chest that was similar to releasing grief. I understood somehow that my body was releasing the guilt I had carried, and this little puppy, carrying the soul of Ralph, was saying, *'It's okay, we're good.'* I knew without a doubt that I had found Ralph and he had come back to help me.

So, Ralph was now Sparky, and Sparky was named by Don *after* he died. That's something I would find hard to believe if I wasn't experiencing this journey myself. Regardless, we were reunited and he was exactly what I needed.

Melanie met Sparky five months after he came into my life. She looked at him and said, "I saw you before you arrived."

The day we met and so happy to have found him.

At the reading when I was told he was coming, Sparky would have been five weeks old. I felt I was missing something, which caused it to take so long to find him, but, in reality, I found him when I was supposed to. When he was old enough to leave his mother.

One piece that didn't make sense was that he was costing me $1,000. I didn't have that amount of money spare. I would never have paid that much money for a puppy. If Don had been alive, we would definitely not have paid $1,000 for a puppy. So why, when the universe and Don teed this up, did they make it a financial burden for me? I used the mortgage money and took him home.

He is perfect, adorable and he melts my heart.
Sitting on the couch at night had been torture because I didn't have Don's to cuddle up to. Sparky made it easier to relax at the end of the day.

Everything happens for a reason. Within a week my son needed $6,000 to pay for surgery for his dog, who had swallowed a nerf ball. Had I not paid for Sparky, I would've given them my mortgage money towards it and scraped by. Don had made me promise in previous readings 'no more money to our children'. So, paying so much for Sparky also insured that I followed through on that promise. Instead, an alternative source of funding appeared for Harley's dog's surgery. And I learned a life lesson.

I knew how essential Sparky's presence was in getting me out of bed every morning. He got me out of the house twice a day for our walks in nature. *Higher Power et al.* was preparing to send me the solution even before I understood I was going to have a problem.

When I thought about sitting on the couch where I met Sparky, and how my life had led me to that point in time, I was in awe. He was the most incredible gift and one of the reasons I survived the most unbearable pain and loneliness.

Naturally, I started to view life as 'before' and 'after'. I looked back and it hurt like hell. I looked forward and it was still not a place I wanted to move toward. The safest space seemed to be right now. It was not necessarily a good place either; it was just better than the other two options.

Then Sparky arrived and insisted I stayed in the now, as in *right now*. When my mind returned to grief, I cried, then he cried too. Reality check – he was only 1.8kg, and I was making him cry. It broke my heart to see him taking on my grief. I questioned whether I got him too soon. He was a distraction, but I still experienced intense grief. Then when I'd had him 2 weeks, he

The vet nurse thought he was adorable and put a lightning bolt on his cast. So cute

broke a bone in his tiny foot while playing with a big dog. Suddenly the maternal instincts were ignited, and I needed to focus on him and care for him more than I needed to focus on my grief. I had questioned why this had happened to Sparky but after, I understood the Universe forced me to tap into my innate nurturing side and it worked.

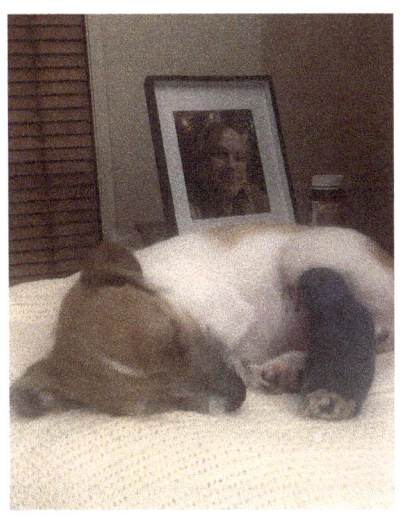

After 2 weeks in his lightning bolt cast, he had to have a new one. No bolt this time, they wanted him discouraged from running around but he had an enthusiasm for life that a cast was not going to interfere with.

Because of his personality, Sparky was also, on occasion, Spartacus. He was fearless, super-friendly and was not intimidated by any dog. He approached every person and dog in the dog park. His Jack Russell/Maltese roots made him calm yet super smart. After he got his cast off, I left the house twice a day to walk him at the dog park. Through him, I met lovely people and made friends. Sparky's outgoing personality reminded me of Don, who would also have been walking, talking and making friends were he still here.

Although I had been told that if I listened, I would hear Don talk to me, I avoided giving it a go. The dog park was full of gum trees with denser forestation down one end. When I took Sparky up one of the trails, I said to Don, "You would have loved this." He responded, "I wouldn't have been able to walk through here, Pam." I burst into tears. It was Don talking. I would never have said that, but I knew the truth of it as soon as he said it.

from my heart to yours...

With hindsight, I can see perfect synchronicity in my past, but trusting life was still not easy at this time. There was so much grief still in me that I was not relaxed, and it was hard to trust completely when tightly wound. Maybe if I'd focused on what would help me relax, I would have started to trust life. *Then*, I would find the peace I had been searching for since Don 'left'.

I do know we are all being looked after, and life manifests in ways we would never have imagined. I wonder if Ralph was Plan B and the baby at forty-six was my Plan A. Had we had the baby, she would have been my distraction and company that Sparky ended up being. But this child was still to be in my life, so she came in as a grandchild.

It reminds me of chess; there are strategic moves being made in our lives at every turn.

Don was not the only one looking out for me, I know. Everyone has passed loved ones and guides helping us every day to bring that perfect synchronicity into our lives. Our job is easy, we just need to trust, relax, follow the signs and let it happen.

*I can't go back
to yesterday,
because I was a
different person then.*

Alice, Alice in Wonderland
Lewis Carroll

20

Carrot number two is a real trip!

22nd October – ten months, eighteen days since Don left this world

Although I had selected a holiday that I knew would be a 'wow' in my future, I didn't feel it. Every time I mentioned the holiday to others, their response was 'wow!', but I was numb even to this. There was no way I would cancel it; I was doing it for my own good. Like it or not! This was an opportunity to heal, transform and prepare myself for the next chapter in my life and, more importantly, so I wouldn't be alone for our wedding anniversary.

Absolutely everything was planned. I just had to get to each point where pickup was already in place. I'm a methodical person so I wasn't worried. But in the taxi on the way to the airport I struggled with being on my own and with the guilt and unfairness of doing something exciting without Don. Luckily, I can cry quietly, and it was dark.

It wasn't long into the trip, however, before I started to experience a strong feeling that I was exactly where I was supposed to be – in a foreign country on my own. I had no anxiety or regrets. In my journal, I liken the feeling to when I went back to see Don the day after I met him. It just felt right! That had been a decision that saw an incredible life unfold for me. So, I had the same feeling of being propelled into this adventure, it felt so right, I didn't question my sanity or isolation. I felt 'go with the flow and it will make sense later'.

When I arrived at the hotel in Chiang Mai, however, I felt lost and alone. I didn't want to stay in the tiny room, and I felt too vulnerable to walk the streets alone. I went downstairs and had a massage in the hotel. That done, I forced myself out and ended up sitting on a tiny veranda/café in torrential rain drinking red wine on my own over the road from the hotel (baby steps). I had dinner and breakfast the next morning in the hotel.

When I arrived at the elephant park the next day, I was introduced to my room mates. A woman from the UK and one from the US. Both were travelling on their own for the first time in their lives. One had lost her husband a couple of years earlier. They were lovely and caring along with the other one hundred and fifty people from all over the world who were volunteering at the park for the week.

This passageway was alongside my room and I had to capture this as a reminder of being in the most incredible place on earth and so close to these magnificent creatures. WOW!

I know you will appreciate that you can still experience deep loneliness amongst one hundred and fifty plus people, regardless of the caring nature of the environment you are in. I was sharing an experience with strangers who I felt separate from. I felt adrift.

The Elephant Nature Park (ENP) is a true humanitarian venture. When I was there, they were caring for over eighty mistreated elephants who carried both physical and emotional scars.

Rescues, however, were not limited to elephants. Lek, the founder, and her team rescued 1,500 dogs when Bangkok flooded in 2011. Dogs not rehomed or reunited with their family were taken to the elephant park in Chiang Mai, where they lived comfortably with many other species of rescued animals, including cats and water buffalo.

Just a few of the approx. 400 cats being cared for at the park.

I was there for the elephants. Helping such magnificent animals who had suffered more than I had, was humbling. It made me feel useful. I was interacting with strangers. I ate vegan food and survived. I had an AUD$7 hour-long massage every night while at the park. I was in the middle of nature and it was serene.

During times when there weren't tasks like working in the elephant kitchen, offloading truckloads of watermelon or bananas, distributing food to the

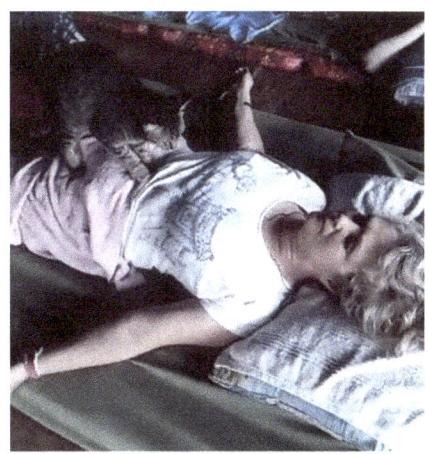

On 3 occassions, massage cat helped with my massage. Feeling very loved and cared for.

enclosures or shovelling elephant poop, or walking rescue dog following surgery, I would take myself somewhere and have a cry, but it was just a short cry. I could see signs I was starting to heal on the inside.

There was no 'real' red wine at the park so I didn't have a wine at the end of the day, as I usually would, although I desperately wanted to so I could feel some connection to my 'normal'. There was, however, a coffee shop, so I could start the next day in the usual way.

Cutting the bananas off the bunch with a machete was not a small job and the picture captures half the bananas

Sometimes, just one bit of normalcy is all you need, and coffee was it for me. But it was also one of the things I missed most with Don's death, our daily coffee at a café.

I went to sleep in a shared room crying silently into Don's t-shirt. On the second morning, I was lining up for my coffee and the lights in the coffee hut started flickering. I knew this was Don. It was just a 'letting you know I'm here' message and that was it. The next morning, I was waiting in line and the 'Perfect' song

Rice being cooked in the elephant kitchen. Nutrients and medicines are added to the rice which is wrapped in banana leaves and fed to the elephants.

Carrot number two is a real trip!

started playing. Don was using his communication skills on the other side of the world while I was getting coffee. He knew this was perfect! I was not alone. I started to relax and appreciate where I was. I was in my wow!

I had taken some of Don's ashes with me with the intention of sprinkling them at the park. I spoke to Lek about this and she volunteered to provide a tree that I could plant with Don's ashes. The thoughtfulness of this gesture was unbelievable. Three days later, two of the staff took me, with Don's ashes and the Poh tree seedling, into the middle of the elephant park and took photos while I planted the tree and Don's ashes.

The first week at the park passed and I was fine. Then I had one night back in Chiang Mai before being picked up the following morning to go to the jungle location. That night I left the hotel and was standing outside a restaurant in the middle of

The tree will eventually be massive and provide shade for these magnificent, rescued mammals.

the markets when someone said my name. It was a volunteer from the park, who I had seen but not really met. We had dinner together. I was getting the hang of this quickly, it seemed.

The second week I was in the jungle with nine volunteers; three of them had been at the park the week before, although I hadn't really met them. Everyone was in their twenties, except me! I could have felt the odd one out, but I didn't. There were two Australians, a Polish couple, two Portuguese sisters from the UK, one Canadian and one American. The camp included cold showers, mattresses on the floor under a mosquito net and vegetarian meals that were served outside.

I was with a group of the most amazing and interesting people, from all over the world, but in the same place as me for this life-changing experience. I laughed more in that week than I had in the last ten months. Laughter, to me, represented normal. I still cried secretly, in bed with Don's t-shirt on my pillow and behind the laundry, but nowhere near as often. I was starting to heal.

We walked for hours to see the elephants in their natural habitat, enjoyed the company of a one-year-old mischievous baby elephant, Gillie, who had a passion for climbing over the fence because she could smell food in our compound. We helped local children with their English homework, helped at a kindergarten where the ENP had provided facilities and lunch once a week, and concreted the floor for a local village recycling centre. It was an unbelievable experience.

I have always known that the best way to raise your spirits is to help another. This trip, and the second week in particular, was exactly what I needed to feel useful, capable, human, and to understand that I could still have an exciting and fun time 'after Don'. My gratitude to the people I shared the jungle week with, Lek and the ENP is immense.

Carrot number two is a real trip!

1 year old Gillie and her Mum who never seemed bothered about our presence so close to her little girl. Maybe she enjoyed the break. Gillie was mischievous and the most hilarious thing in my life has been watching her repeatedly climb over the barrier to get in and out of our compound.

Don made his presence known just enough to help me relax, and I have no doubt he shared every experience with me.

After the jungle week, I had one night back at the park and then one night in Chiang Mai before flying home. This was a unique experience. So many firsts. So, I suppose it is no surprise that I came home with a tattoo as well.

On the last trip from the ENP to Chiang Mai, Amelia was telling Lindsay about a tattoo shop in Chiang Mai, owned by an Australian where she had her tattoo done. It was not far from where we were being dropped off. Lindsay was going to get a tattoo that afternoon and I was sitting in the van vacillating about getting one, although I didn't say anything out loud.

Just before we arrived at our destination, 'Perfect' started playing in the van. Was that support from the other side? Yes. Don was telling me, *'Do it!'* I had second thoughts, again while sitting in the tattoo shop waiting area, until a white bird swooped down and flew across the front of the glass windows. Okay.

The tattoo is on my right wrist so I can wear a bracelet over it if I choose. It has angel wings and the words 'She flies with her own wings'. A reminder in permanent ink!

In my thirties, I had seriously considered getting a tattoo on my right shoulder blade of a green tree frog looking behind 'us' over his right shoulder. When it became more popular to have a tattoo, I lost interest.

Although I had been working *with* Don for much of my work life, I was never working *for* Don. Then, in the last ten years, I was 'spreading my wings' so to speak, and rising in positions within organisations on my own steam. In the year before Don died, I felt the urge to get a tattoo of 'She flies with her own wings'. Surprisingly, Don also thought it was a great idea. I think we were both getting a sense that this was where life was taking me/us.

I had always planned to design my own tattoo before getting it done. So this one wasn't a breadcrumb on our path, it was a seed planted in my mind so that when I had to fly with my own wings, the concept was not new, there was a rightness and familiarity to it. To get this tattoo at the end of a volunteer holiday where I didn't just fly, I soared, was just another experience that showed me I was going to be okay. I had this!

I had such an incredible experience and decided I would return with our children on Don's next birthday, which coincidently would also be the second anniversary of his death. They would experience caring on a whole new level, see Don's tree and hopefully we could place a plaque for him on the fence.

Don was the kindest, most incredibly caring person. His ashes, under a tree providing shade to rescued elephants who were being cared for to the end of their life, was an incredibly special and fitting tribute to a wonderful man.

Carrot number two is a real trip!

And going home was made better because Sparky was waiting for me.

from my heart to yours . . .

The absolute best parts of life post Don were the two carrots I placed in my future: Sparky and the Elephant Nature Park.

He's a character!

Sparky watches TV with me but is too vocal if the program has animals in it, even cartoons! Consequently, he has been banned from watching David Attenborough documentaries.

Sparky also likes to sing. He has 2 songs in his repertoire 'Leave a light on' by Tom Walker and 'Girls like you' by Maroon 5. He has also added Ambulance sirens to his repertoire but that's just embarrassing.

I needed Sparky for company. I really cannot comprehend the loneliness I would have endured had I not had this constant companion. I also needed to still give and receive love so that I could begin to heal. He helped dissolve some of the numbness I carried in my heart. He filled my days with his enthusiasm for life.

The volunteer holiday wasn't easy, and it was only my determination that got me there. When you run a marathon, you prepare, you build up your resilience and stamina. This is what I had been doing, ever so slowly, since Don died; taking steps forward in my life in small ways and building up until I did something that shocked my family and friends because it was big and I was doing it alone. This carrot showed me how strong I really was.

Plan your wow. You deserve it! You can do it. You've got this!

I found so much joy and peace in helping others. It still warms my heart to see a genuine smile on my face at this stage in my grieving. Thank you, Elephant Nature Park!

*And in the end,
it's not the years in
your life that count.
It's the life in your years.*

Abraham Lincoln

21

Twelve months – focus on the life, not the death

4th December – twelve months since Don left this world

What do you do when you approach the twelve-month mark? Is it our culture that creates this need to acknowledge the passing of a calendar year? Regardless, the thought of Don's last day on Earth being celebrated or ignored were both unacceptable.

Because I tend to look, as much as possible, for the positive, I came to find it oddly comforting that Don's birthday was the day after he died. We could therefore celebrate his birthday, while acknowledging his absence. This left everyone to deal with the day before his birthday on their own terms.

To ensure Don's birthday celebrated his impact on our lives, I set a requirement for the birthday dinner. Using the alphabet, I asked for as many examples of unique life experiences with Don as possible. It was 'homework', so, true to form, our daughter generated a list for every letter of the alphabet, and I helped our son with his list (eyeroll). I also had my own list.

Dinner was at our friendly local Italian restaurant, Mama Mia's, where Don and the owner had bonded because of their propensity for inappropriate conversation. It seemed a fitting place to celebrate events that made us laugh because they were unique Don events.

Some memories were on everyone's lists, but there were so many unique stories that kept everyone entertained for hours.

It was immediate family, but we could have invited anyone who knew Don because everyone had a 'Don story'. He made experiences memorable for so many people.

Some of my favourites:

- A = Accepting of others. Don was kind and helped anyone he could. In the early 1990s a man approached him for a job because he had heard Don on a radio interview and wanted to work for him. The guy was unskilled and earning his living unlawfully; however, he had a baby girl and wanted her to be proud of him when she was older. Don created a job for him so he could make the life change he wanted.

- B = Bowtie. Over a period of several months Don 'nagged/encouraged' our favourite café to add lambs fry and bacon to their breakfast menu. They finally succumbed and announced it would be available that coming weekend. Don arrived for breakfast wearing a white shirt and bowtie to give it the appropriate level of importance it deserved. It was hilarious.

- D = Dirty Dick's Night Cart. While running a theatre restaurant called Dirty Dicks in the early 1980s, Don recognised the danger of people drinking and driving and offered a ride-home service. The van was called Dirty Dick's Night Cart (Don humour – refer Victorian times night carts). This was decades before designated drivers or alternative transport became the done thing.

- D = Dog fights. Our son encouraged Don to join a gaming squadron that engaged in WWII dog fights using planes with accurate flying capability and specifications. Don was over seventy at this time and managed to accumulate more planes, through skill, than other squad members who were at least two generations younger and avid gamers.

♡ F = Fire pole. When we renovated an old house, Don advised the builder he wanted a fire pole installed between the kids' study upstairs and the dining room downstairs. The builder looked to me asking, "Is he serious?" Yep. Then when the hole was cut in the ceiling, Don advised, "Not big enough – I need to fit through as well."

♡ G = Grandmothers. Don flirted with older ladies (friends' mothers or grandmothers) and called them his girlfriends. They loved him for the time and attention he gave them and for making them feel special again.

♡ S = Searchlight. Don bought a WWII searchlight with about fifty years' supply of carbon rods (power supply). After restoring it, he had the only operating searchlight in New Zealand (because he could). He exported the excess carbon rods to US searchlight enthusiasts with no import tax as they were American products. The profit from the sale of the rods back to the US was considerably more than what he had paid for the searchlight.

♡ T = Terrific. Part of Don's ritual when dropping the kids at school was, they had responded to Don's 'What is your day going to be like today?' with a fist pump and 'terrific'. Stacey's enthusiasm as a teenager was sadly lacking but she did it. I'm sure they will both do this with their own children.

♡ W = Wall of death. Don had been a speedway rider and had always wanted to ride the wall of death. In 1989 he arranged for the wall to be part of a lifestyle show/fair we organised, and he got his opportunity. At the age of forty-six, over twice the age of the riders on the circuit, he successfully rode the wall on his first try.

♡ W = Waterbed. We had a king-size waterbed for many years. On numerous occasions if I climbed into bed after Don was already in there, he would throw himself off the other side and land on the floor as if I had caused a tidal wave. He was so funny!

from my heart to yours...

Every time we turned a difficult time into a celebration of Don's life, we created another special memory instead of pain.

On one particular day, when Stacey was feeling the loss of her dad, she shared a funny photo of Don on Facebook. She was then encouraged to post a new photo of him every day, and this became a posting of Don's 'making life fun' pictures, like Don having fun in the pool. This was great because friends and family wanted to enjoy these moments as well and the commentary on the posts was just wonderful.

Later she set up a specific FaceBook page to

This is what happens when Don has to entertain himself in the pool.

Twelve months – focus on the life, not the death

This is the hole that Don dug.

Don called Harley from the bottom of the hole because he was stuck in the mud and he wanted Harley to hand him the spade he couldn't reach. Looks like Harley's contemplating some payback for times when Don had fun at Harley's expense.

Not all Don's fun was shared. Harley was too small to drive and is not impressed with Dad's level of enjoyment.

honor Don's memory called Don Appreciation Group (D.A.G). On this Facebook page, people also posted photos on their own or in groups, toasting Don on his birthday.

The photo of, what was referred to as 'Don's hole' is indicative of his propensity for generating fun in the most unlikely places. He would start a project, and engage people in the process with hilarious posts on FB. In this instance he had to dig down to unearth a broken water pipe in an easement. This could only be done by hand. So Don dug the hole, on his own, at 70 years of age.

Trevor Harding, a lifelong friend, posted this photo on the FB page. They had been friends for almost 60 years and had met on the speedway track in Perth in their late teens. Trevor, a legend on the circuit, always wore white leathers and is still affectionately called Ghosty.

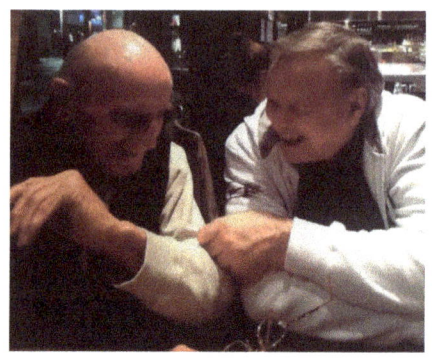

The best of mates for life!

I love this picture because this is what conversations with Don looked like. He laughed and created a ripple of laughter everywhere he went.

Quite often in conversations, since his passing, someone would slip in a 'dad' joke so we could all acknowledge that Don would have said that, and it would start a funny dialogue of shared memories.

The game we played on his birthday could be done in so many ways, on Facebook or at family gatherings.

Remember, your loved one is always within reach. Say their name, set a place for them, or pour their favourite drink at special occasions; they'll be there.

Our universe grants every soul a twin – a reflection of themselves, the kindred spirit – and no matter where they are or how far away they are from each other – even if they are in different dimensions – they will always find one another. This is destiny; this is love.

Julie Dillon

22

"What! How can you have left me again?"

8th December – twelve months, four days since Don left this world

Although I handled Don's first departure from this life through a filter of shock, I did have a clear understanding of what had happened. It was, without question, Don's time to go.

He was never going to live forever, and marriage vows assure us it's 'till death do us part'. I also have a firm understanding that he is still with me.

When I introduced Andy in Chapter 1, I mentioned that he had communicated with his dad for six months after he had died. Andy communicates with people in spirit after they have gone through healing and before they go to a higher vibration (home). He refers to the place they are in as the Boarding House and describes it in detail.

Time in the Boarding House obviously varies for individuals, as Annette indicated they move on after three months, whereas Andy's dad was there for six months. I wasn't monitoring the time for Don in this place because I had no concept of where specifically he was, other than it was all on the other side. This was new territory for me. As long as I could communicate with him, the label for the space didn't matter.

I went to see Andy on 8th December, as it was twelve months since Don had died and six months since my last visit to him. I was struggling. I struggled every day so was horrified when I found I could struggle more. I wanted some grief lifted, but I also wanted to connect with Don. The last session had been exceptional where my system had been flooded with Don's love. A shared experience post death that was now a precious memory added to the list.

As soon as the session started, Andy advised there was a man there that wasn't Don. He described him. It sounded like the guy was dressed for golf. I said I didn't know who this would be. WTF! This stranger had come forward just to let me know Don had moved on. I choked. Tears ran down my face for the full forty-five minutes of the healing session. I was devastated, again.

I always thought I was fortunate that I understood Don was still there. I thought it would be unbearable to think your loved one was lost to you forever. So, I was totally unprepared for the pain of losing him *again.*

We never intentionally hurt the other, but I felt like Don had just broken up with me by SMS (Stranger Messenger Service). That hurt. Why could I not have been prepared for this? Given a heads up? Why would he say he would be with me to the end of my life then leave without warning?

During the session, Andy told me I was in the middle of a big wooden bridge, built by the Master Carpenter. My past was behind me. Ahead of me was infinity fog. You could not see through it. It required trust, faith and surrender.

He went on to say, that I needed to know I had done nothing wrong. That I was in the right place. That my feet were what moved me forward, so I needed to focus on energy

"What! How can you have left me again?"

healing that was centred around my feet like grounding and reflexology.

Feeling I had in some way held up job opportunities and healing was a constant for me even though I had been told repeatedly I could not get it wrong and I was exactly where I was supposed to be. This message is exactly what I needed to hear but I was so consumed by Don's absence it only made sense later when I reviewed my journal notes.

After the session, I was so distraught about Don. I sent the following SMS to Don's mobile number. It hadn't been in service for a long time, but sometimes I found comfort in texting him.

Gutted, Don.

Just when I think I'm getting to the end of this... maybe. You derail me. That's not fair.

If you were here, I would be putting antlers on the car and thinking it was funny. I don't seem to have that in me anymore.

How is it that you were able to take so much of me with you? I thought 'I' was solid and mine and not something someone could take from me. But you did. And I feel betrayed on top of that because you are gone (again) and I don't know what that means. I went to Andy for healing. To take a step forward and instead I fell off a cliff.

I also sent an SMS to Melanie, our psychic friend, advising what had happened. Melanie said, "WHAT! We'll see about that!"

I received a clear message in my head saying, 'Think it through.' So, I did.

 Don said he would always be with me and I believed him.

 Melanie regularly connected with people who had been gone longer than twelve months, so was it only Andy that could no longer connect with Don?

I picked up seven feathers instead of the usual one when I walked Sparky around the streets the day before.

Were the feathers a parting gift or Don's way of saying, *'You need to remember I'm still with you?'* I believe it was the latter. He knew I had this heartache coming and was reinforcing his continued presence, knowing I would need it! Because I was just so damn emotional about everything now!

Melanie also came back to me and confirmed he was still within reach.

It was so easy to fall back into the 'I can't believe you left me' whirlpool. But I knew the statement was from my human mind. It was my conscious (ego) saying, if you can't see him, he's not here. My soul and the spiritual side of me knew he wouldn't leave. On that level, we couldn't be separated.

from my heart to yours...

Getting a message at this time about trust, faith and surrender was actually everything I was pushing against. I was constantly looking at how I could take control when really that just created feelings of dissatisfaction with what I had and judgement of what I had.

Ironically, it is the act of 'taking control' that reinforces you don't have it. The moment you let go, you are back in control again.

I used to view life as a game of strategy, but at this moment it was real, and although I wanted to toss the Monopoly board into the air and storm off, it was not that sort of game. Every card in my deck was saying, *'Suck it up, sunshine.'*

Trust, faith and surrender is the key to finding the peace I was looking for.

We need to live life knowing our loved one is there, but not failing to live because we are so focused on their death. I know it is not as easy as it sounds. One day at a time and self-care above all else.

Life is a balance between letting go and holding on.

Rumi

23
It's clearer to see where I am now!

3rd May – sixteen months and twenty-nine days since Don left this world

I felt stuck, again. I wondered if there was ever going to be a time I felt like my life was just flowing again. One day, when I felt low, I was finishing a midday entry in my journal to try to clear my head and I heard lyrics on the radio *that were a message from Don saying he would be there for me.* Thank you, Don.

I booked a session with Melanie and Don for the next day, to get some direction.

Melanie told me she was not getting a sense that the house would be sold. But also told me the next place would be on water and on a ground floor. Great, one less thing to worry about because I was absolutely not going to worry about where the money for that would come from!

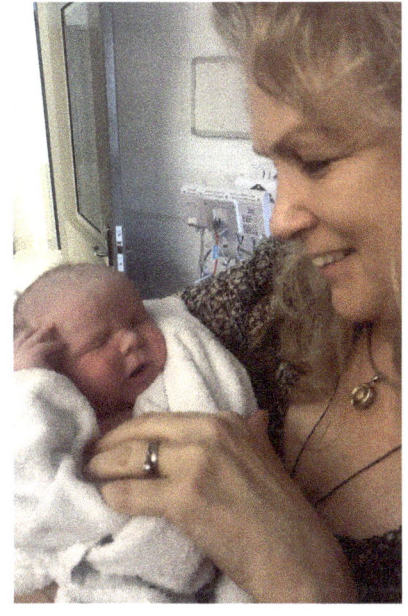

She talked about the job that would come my way. *Great! Looking forward to it and I'll need it so I can pay for this 'next place'!*

Melanie then talked about the birth of our first grandchild, which was six weeks previously. She said, "Don was at the birth!" WOW! I wasn't far behind him. I got to hold her when she was only hours old.

This baby's soul was special to him (us) and was previously mentioned as 'it' was present in readings with Don and Ralph. Melanie was telling me that Don was seeing her through to start her life here – this really was mind-blowing.

I had felt alone in this world, although I wasn't, but this reinforced the strong connections we have *outside* of our physical life. Both Ralph/Sparky and Lilly had come into my life as blessings. How could I not feel looked after when so much of what had been orchestrated would help me through this horrendous event.

I was told that the baby was a lovely spirit and she would have a strong love connection with me. There would be lots of babysitting (I can confirm she melts my heart, and from three months of age, we have had sleepovers *every Friday night* – she is a massive blessing in my life).

My blessings. They were exactly what I needed. Thank you.

In the first reading I'd had with Annette she advised that after about three months, communication is more difficult. It was now over sixteen months since Don died, and I was not getting a sense of distance. He was still sending messages, so I asked Melanie, 'What does that mean?' She explained that Don's vibration had raised, but he had helped me raise mine as well so there was no greater distance between us. That was a relief! Don had it under control!

Don was reiterating what he said every reading, but I seemed to need reminding that *he would never leave me*. He also said that he was guiding me. Melanie said he was showing a net in the water and the fish swimming as he was guiding it forward.

He acknowledged in the reading that I cried a lot. He was actually the *only one* who knew how much I cried. He also told me he watched over me from the landing. That was so fitting; it was his spot when he was here because it was just outside his office door and overlooked the lounge, dining room and kitchen.

Melanie said she could see me travelling. Yes, to New Zealand and Thailand. She told me not to worry about the New Zealand trip, I would be okay. This trip was to see both our families, and it would be the first time back in New Zealand without Don. So many shared memories are in New Zealand and people I have only known when I was part of 'us'.

Don was telling me through Melanie that I would find a book on our bookshelf, when I was ready, that had a bookmark in it. It would be relevant to what I needed to know, 'when I am ready'. I was told not to look for it yet, but we have over 500 books so I was happy to wait for 'when I'm ready'.

Back at home I was hearing the song 'Healing hands' by Conrad Sewell. I felt Don's energy in the song, and he seemed to be saying I had healing hands. Was this because I hoped to be working for a humanitarian organisation (my life needed to have a purpose now) and I had quit my job three days before, so there would be a new job? Or was he talking about *us* because the lyrics that also resonated said he would never let go? I think it was the latter because he kept reaffirming that he would never leave me, and I knew he had some difficult times in his life before I arrived. I also knew that, with time, hindsight would eventually answer this question. It's like wanting to read the last page of a book. I wanted to know now so I could put current events into perspective, but I had to be patient.

I had recently had a session with another friend who was a reiki healer and numerologist. She gave me insight into the relevance of my life number (I never really understood this before but now I was interested).

I highly recommend the book *The Life You Were Born to Live* by Dan Millman, which provides a comprehensive view of life numbers and the impact they have. It provides some insight into how to navigate your life path.

To calculate your life number, your date of birth – expressed as individual digits – is added together to give you a double digit. This number is then added together to give you a single digit, which is your Life Purpose.

For example, a date of birth of 18/09/1961 is expressed as 1+8+0+9+1+9+6+1 = 35 then 3+5 = 8.

My number is 35/8. The first numbers represent the attributes you have that will either help you or hinder you (depending on whether the trait is expressed negatively or positively) on your journey to achieve your Life Purpose – for me that is an 8 (3 is Expression and Sensitivity, 5 is Freedom and Discipline, 8 is Influence and Abundance). Looking at Don's life number has the benefit of being able to view a completed life, as he was no longer a work-in-progress. Don is 25/7 (2 is Cooperation and Balance, 5 is Freedom and Discipline and 7 is Trust and Openness).

When his life finished and he went 'home', we were told that Don didn't require much healing. But did this also mean he completed what he set out to do when he planned this life?

I look at his number with more interest than mine. I can see cooperation, balance, discipline and freedom in his life. Did he achieve the trust and openness he was aiming for before he died? Yes.

In first reviewing the characteristics of Don's life number, I felt confused because his number seemed to portray a character that was the opposite of Don. Only in looking back to the person he was when we met did I start to appreciate the changes he made in his life that I was witness to.

I know he didn't trust as easily at the beginning, as would be common when people have had broken relationships. Six years after we met, we lost a lot of money in business. Don admitted that he expected I would leave him because we had nothing. This wasn't about me, but what he was here to learn. Through some challenging times, he learned that he could trust me to be beside him no matter what happened in our life.

My *healing hands* helped him by simply providing unconditional love and support. I feel he left this life with the challenges in his life number successfully completed. He was calm and he flowed with life. He didn't carry anger, hatred, regret or guilt baggage with him. Well done, Don!

Astrology for the Soul by Jan Spiller was the bookmarked book I was told to find. One night I just wanted to know why I was struggling so much and went in search of 'the book'. Don had previously commented on my choice of reading material, so although we had over 500 books, I figured it was a safe assumption I wasn't looking for a romance novel. I found the book in the self-help, new-age section and I'd bookmarked information on my North Node. This is another indicator of the challenges you will face and is based on your date of birth and astrology. It identifies attributes you need to develop and those you need to leave behind. It was insightful on why I struggle with certain aspects of life. I relooked at what I needed to *develop* (self-confidence, taking risks, having fun, developing an 'it's up to me' attitude) and what I needed to *leave behind* (detaching from emotional situations, waiting for others to prompt my actions, running away from confrontations, aloofness). I was sitting very snuggly back with my *'leave behind'* tendencies, and I can also appreciate that I had all the *develop* aspects ticked off before Don had died. There were now skid marks back to where I started!

Since Don died, I could see I had lost confidence and courage and was back to traits I had previously overcome. That's why I was struggling. That's why I wasn't the person I was.

I am open to any new perspective on life. It had been so hard for so long that I didn't want to struggle if I could help it. Looking at my Life Number and North Node gave me perspective on challenges and something to work on. Effectively, I was looking at my life with its massive challenges and seeing them instead in terms of single steps to complete.

Don was well prepared for his trip home. I will be too!

from my heart to yours...

Keep moving forward and when you stumble or take a step back, as you will inevitably do at times, stop, look at where you are compared to where you started and say, "This pause/hiccup/catastrophe doesn't really matter so much because *look at how far I've come!*"

So, what can we learn from Don? If you carry emotions of regret, anger or guilt, do what you can to get rid of them. They are the emotions that can fester. There is no shortcut with grief, so do yourself a favour and work on releasing the other emotions that are going to make your life even harder. Choose to let them go.

If you are struggling with something in life, especially if an issue is recurring, look at your birth number and those of the people closest to you. It can really help you understand what's going on for you and others. When I recognised what was recurring in my life, I changed my reaction to it next time it happened, so I had a greater chance of the lesson not repeating again.

What soap is to the body; laughter is to the soul.

Yiddish proverb

24

"OMG Don, did you just make me laugh?"

22nd June – eighteen months and eighteen days since Don left this world

Life was challenging before I lost Don, but I had balance because I was in a relationship that meant there was always something good in my life!

I had quit my job at the end of April and had remained unemployed for too long, far longer than I expected. I expected to take two to three weeks between jobs, but now it had been almost two months. Don was gone; there was no other income. And I had perimenopause. The main loss I felt at this stage was not having Don to share the bad times, a problem shared… I was carrying a deep sadness that seemed to be my new default setting.

One day, a currawong was sitting in the outside area. I tried to shoo him away but that was ineffective, so I went inside. The next day he returned, stood on the outside table and picked up a long screw that had fallen out of the packet. I shooed him but, same result, I went inside and took a photo of him through the window. When he was ready, he flew away, so I went and put the screw back in the packet and left it on the table. They were a reminder of a job I had to do so couldn't put them out of sight.

The next day when the currawong returned, he hopped along the outside table, picked a long screw *out of the packet* with his beak, hopped onto the chair and, with the screw in his beak, started banging it on the back of the chair. It was hilarious. Very comic! Without conscious thinking, I just blurted out, "Is that you, Don?"

The bird hopped onto the top of my swing chair and started singing beautifully. I was so taken with his performance I didn't get a photo of him banging the chair with the screw but did capture him during his song. The bird never came back to perform again but I swear I felt Don's energy. At the next reading, I intended to ask Don about the comedic currawong.

It was the sort of thing Don would do; if he wanted me to laugh, he would find a way. He would be relentless in his pursuit of my laughter. This event in particular I wanted to remember to ask him about.

OMG Don, did you just make me laugh?"

I'd also had a butcher bird entertain us as it cheekily kept picking at Sparky's bone every time Sparky walked away from it. This went on for probably an hour. In the end Sparky took it away and buried it.

The next day I carried my granddaughter outside, and the butcher bird landed on a chair back no more than two feet from us and started singing. This bird, now called Bertie, came most days, but it wasn't until I realised he always showed up when my daughter, son or granddaughter were with me, that reinforced Bertie was carrying Don's energy. He came back almost every day for about three months.

One day, Sparky and I went to a different dog park that was much bigger. When we arrived, the carpark was almost full, and I backed into a space. I would normally drive in nose first and have no idea why I didn't on this day. When we returned to the car an hour later, most of the parks were empty, including the one on the driver's side of my car. In that space was a bright blue spiky rubber ball. Not the usual tennis ball left at dog parks, but a special toy. Don always said I would recognise his energy in things. Without thinking, I picked it up and handed it to Sparky. "I think this is for you," I told him. To Don I said, "I think it's too big."

Sparky loves the green ball. It's perfect! And faded and chewed! The blue ball was too big and is never played with.

It still surprises me when I get validation that Don's energy was in things like the ball. I had no doubt. The next day we went to a shopping centre and I parked on the far end of the carpark under the trees. I usually park closer to the doors but on this day I didn't – just an unexplained change in habit.

But on my walk back to the car I went through the multitude of empty car spaces and three-quarters of the way back to the car, in my direct path, was a green spiky ball, identical to the blue one but smaller. That wasn't a coincidence. That was Don! And parking in a different spot was no accident either.

I knew Don's personality and therefore could see it in the random things that happened. I also never doubted when I felt something had his mark on it.

from my heart to yours...

You may not experience the same things I did but remember the personality of the person you have lost, the things that were important to you, and keep your eyes and ears open. Trust your intuition even on seemingly unimportant things.

A friend of mine who had also lost her husband went to a coffee shop with relatives soon after his sudden death. When the coffees were delivered there was an extra one. Exactly what her husband would have ordered. He was letting them know he was there.

In another reading, Don said 'cup and saucer'. That's it! He offered no further context. When I was younger, I used to only drink tea from a cup and saucer. In any other vessel it tasted wrong. Then, whenever something happened, Don would straight away make a cup of tea. We would stop, step back from a situation for a bit and just find peace with each other. But what did he mean? There was no context, only my musings on what the words meant to me.

A month later, a friend of Don's, who was shifting overseas, offered me a cup and saucer she wasn't taking with her. She had two others but didn't want the one with February on it and forget-me-not flowers. Immediately I *knew* this was from Don. Valentine's month and forget-me-nots. I sit and drink tea from this cup several times a day. Sometimes to take a break and step back from 'life' for a bit, but mostly because, like the word game at night, it is a connection. He was the most incredibly thoughtful man and still is.

I said early on I was looking for peace, I have found peace in this simple act of stopping for a cup of tea in this special cup. I know he is with me; I feel it. It was the perfect gift.

Why was he cryptic? Because he had told me through Melanie (Chapter 26) that I would find a gift from him in Thailand, but I didn't. I was so frantic about finding it and being able to afford it, I never saw what I was to find. He made sure this time I couldn't overthink it.

A couple of weeks later I was given the other two cup and saucer sets as well. Because Don's message was in the February cup, I received that on its own so there was no mistaking Don's message.

I don't try to convince someone else that something is a message and not a coincidence. I see it for the personal gift and special memory that it is. When you receive a message from the other side, it is for you. It's personal. It's love.

*I lost my way
all the way to you
and in you I found
the way back to me.*

Atticus

25

Third time is a charm

28th June – eighteen months and twenty-four days since Don left this world

I knew he had gone but I wanted to share my problems with Don again, even though I knew it wasn't the same. Don understood me, sometimes more than I understood myself. So, I booked another session with Annette for guidance and to talk to Don. The last session with Annette had been twenty days after Don died, now it was almost twenty months!

Annette was chosen for the first reading with Don because Amanda, Stacey's friend had come forward in a reading with Annette, whereas she had never come forward before. Prior to that I had been to Annette for readings about my career and now I was in the same situation of wanting to know what job was coming and when. I was also going to communicate with Don.

As usual, Don was in the session as soon as we started. Annette described him as beautiful and peaceful.

She started straight off asking me whether I'd found the insurance. I said, "No."

This read more like a movie script. From the first conversation through mediums with Don, he had told me there was insurance money. But I hadn't found anything and was confused about it, so I haven't referred to it when recounting previous readings, but it kept coming up.

We had no communication problems when he was alive, and even though he was 'dead' it still upset me that we were not in sync with communication on this. I know it seems weird. It was like, what did I expect?

Annette asked Don for more information. He referred to me as 'my darling' and referenced the insurance. It was unbelievably comforting to hear those words of endearment, even if it was through someone else. Annette sighed and described Don as a sweetheart. I wished I could see everything she saw.

It was funny about the insurance because I had gone to the bank several times asking about insurance. I had to tell them that I'd been instructed there was some insurance, please look again. This was not the time to tell them my dead husband was the one telling me. Ha-ha, right?

One of the main reasons for this session was for me to understand where my next job was, as it hadn't come yet and I was getting desperate. Nothing I did seemed to be working for me in this respect. I felt like I was stuck between the life *we* had and *my* independent life. I wanted to know what I could do.

Annette said, "There's a part of you that hasn't recognised your own potential because of the role Don had in your life." She paused and was listening to something I couldn't hear. She said, "You have been left here to walk your own path, but you are not trusting in your own abilities. You're second-guessing yourself." Oops, nailed it!

She said that I (Pam) knew Don was a visionary and trusted him so much to lead the way. I needed to know that I was very much a visionary as well but had just not had the opportunity to see my own path without him there.

She reiterated that Don was sweeping the path in front of me and the rest was up to me. He had swept it but I was not seeing it yet, which was pretty normal, she said, but it was now about me trusting in my own self and not needing Don to lead the way.

Annette went on to say that we all go through the chapters of our journey. Nothing we do is by accident or wrong. It is all supposed to happen. Even the unpleasant things. We may regret things, but we can't go back there. We can't change what has happened, only the thoughts we have about what happened. This last piece I deeply believe and have had the following as a little e-card on my desk for years:

"When you change the way you look at things, the things you look at change."

Dr. Wayne Dyer

I also wanted to understand why I hadn't seen him when I had been repeatedly told he would show himself to me. I asked whether I had lost that opportunity to see him through grieving for so long? She reiterated, "No, you never lose an opportunity," and went on to say that energy from meditation makes it easier for them to reach us as it puts our vibration above the density of our existence here.

There was more said about my path but after a while I realised Don hadn't said anything for ages. That was unusual so I asked if he was still there. She said that today he was on my right. Although he was usually on my left, today there were other guides on my left. I found myself leaning to my right after I knew where he was. Leaning was a way of being closer, if that was at all possible. Don was in my heart; you can't get much closer than that!

What Annette went on to explain I feel are generalisations relevant to most people, so I have included them. Don insisted in every reading that he would never leave my side, and I trusted him on that. These points do provide some clarity on what to expect though:

1. After about three months they shift to a higher vibration where they won't be seeing everything we do.

2. Annette explained that a thought will bring a loved one closer. Imagine they are in another room that we can't come into until we've passed over. The entrance to that room comes closer to us. But a thought will bring them through.

3. They will also come on special occasions, and it will be easier for them as it won't be the thick dense energy of us *needing* them to be there.

I was finding I needed to be more specific when I wanted the answer to come directly from Don. I asked whether he still stood on the landing. Annette said, "Yes, he does."

I explained to Annette that there used to be butterflies, birds and songs, but now I wasn't sure whether there were messages, and Sparky hadn't barked at the landing for a long time. She advised he was still as close but not to my physical self. I didn't understand but I moved on.

I felt confident that I could get an answer regarding the bird mentioned in the previous chapter, so I asked whether this was Don.

Annette advised that birds represent freedom. They're flying high. That's symbolic of them going through healing. It's part of their transformation. She said he hadn't gone into that bird, but his energy had.

I asked again, "Was it him?"

Annette asked, "Did the bird look at you?"

I said, "Yes, the whole time he was there."

I realised I was still only getting answers from Annette, so I asked her to ask Don. I wanted *his* answer to the question (doh!). She said he was just grinning, nodding and saying, "She knows that it was."

This response was classic Don and perfect, *that's* what I needed! Now I had another memory that didn't just make me smile; I laughed out loud when I saw in my mind's eye the comedic actions of this bird. A bird I could see Don's personality in. Isn't that incredible!

While I'm proofreading this part of the book, lyrics come through loudly from downstairs: about flying like a bird and likening it to having died and gone to heaven. He's so funny!

One of the main reasons I went to readings was to get snippets that helped me feel connected and closer to Don. It was these bits of communication from him that I carried with me. Annette said again, "He is a very beautiful, peaceful soul. Don's saying, 'This is part of her journey and she chose it anyway.'"

This was another situation where he was responding to what I had said to him when alone. I had said, "I know that I wrote my journey and so I wrote losing you into my life plan."

I said to Don, "I understand."

Annette started to explain something, but I advised it was a joke. Don used to say that to us just to shut us up. Annette said he was laughing at that. It lightened my heart and made me smile. Finally, I was hearing more from Don.

A lot of the reading had been on my job and finances, and Annette's answers usually came through her guides, so logically, I suppose, Don was on the sideline on these discussions. But now

I needed him in the forefront. She had already told me about the job, now I was only here to talk to Don.

Don went on to say, "As I look back now, I perhaps could have paved the way for this. To give her more of a feel for her choosing her direction a bit more."

I said, "Looking back, we wouldn't have changed anything. We had a great life."

But yes, I could see how the way we lived made my transition to solo more difficult, but only in this respect. I never initiated a change, I was living with an entrepreneur, dammit! Our life was an incredible adventure led by Don's personality, innovative mindset and courage. I wouldn't change anything and therefore just needed to deal with these challenging times.

Don was showing Annette someone on my left side – Kathryn – and introducing her as one of my guides, but I was advised she was not someone I knew in this lifetime. I was told to call upon Kathryn when I felt unsupported or lonely. I hoped Kathryn wasn't busy because this was how I usually felt. As I tended to call on Don a lot, I suppose indirectly I was being told to give him a break. I would call Kathryn; she was my guide (but I would still speak to Don).

I had never been given a name for my guide before and so I asked whether our guides change. I was advised we have different guides for different stages in our life, and the more my vibration rose, the higher the entity was that came to guide me.

Annette advised that Don couldn't be my guide because in this lifetime it had been the relationship. He could guide me, as in sweep the path, but everything I did was ultimately a separate energy now. For me, he may be dead, but he was an integral part of my life and the connection was ongoing.

She said, "When your time comes, he will be there to show you the way over. He says, '*I love you*, but I don't want you to be here. I know you have so much to do.'"

I believed he was saying this because I had said to *him* so many times that I would rather just join him, but Annette didn't know that. Plus, this was the first reading where '*I love you*' had been communicated verbatim. Thank you!

Annette said Don was showing 'V' for victory with his fingers and was telling me it was all going to be better than okay. She said he was a wise old soul. This was interesting to hear as he had felt when we were both here that my soul was older. I think this is because although we were both accepting of our changing spiritual beliefs, I was more open or intuitive to what it meant. In reality, it was probably because I had eighteen years less social conditioning than Don to untangle from what we are directed to believe, almost from birth. Regardless, this way round, with him going first, my openness had allowed for so much more communication between us in our respective places. Everything happens for a reason!

Annette confirmed I'd had more than one lifetime with this man and sometimes roles were reversed. We are both old souls.

She went on to say that something happened in Don's last lifetime that led to his sometimes-non-acceptance or difficulty accepting some things. I understood this because Don had so much courage and conviction that he kept his focus when told something couldn't be done and proved naysayers wrong. One time in particular, he made a decision he held fast on but later regretted, then questioned himself on why he had taken such a strong stand that ultimately wasn't in his interests. I could see these reactions reflected in what Annette was saying had come through from his last life.

I said, "He always felt he had been a fighter pilot in WWII, possibly German. He had always wanted a Rolex Oyster, so when he didn't want a wedding ring, I used every cent I had to buy him the Rolex Oyster as an alternative wedding band. In addition, since Don's death, I've been told that the Rolex Oyster was given to British pilots in WWII, so if Don had been a German pilot then he may have always wanted one in his previous life. It seems to me his deep desire for a Rolex Oyster could be another connection between his last life and this one."

Don was then passing information on this through Annette.

"He says, 'I did learn a lot in that lifetime, some of it was lessons, some blessings. I came back in very quickly, I died in 1942, shot down by the English, and came back in 1943.'"

This is interesting because Don was named after his uncle who was a POW being held by the Germans at the time Don was born. If Don had been German, it would place his past-life personality on opposing sides with his uncle, prior to dying in that life.

Don asked Annette to ask me, "Did you want to know if he was English or German?"

I said, "He originally thought he was English but had more affinity with the German planes so guessed he was probably German."

Don then confirmed he had been a German pilot but had an English father and a German mother and had been born an Englishman. He said he was a bit rebellious and gravitated to his mother's family who were still in Germany. That's how he ended up in the German Air Force. Don told me his name was Richard in that life (I'm sure if I tried hard enough, I could find him in archives). To clarify, this was not one of the lives I had shared with Don.

Don said his father in his last life was ashamed that he ended up in the German military. Then he said, "I was too, until now." Because he flew for Germany, he was not recognised as a war hero by England, his own country. He said, "I've processed that, as part of my healing, in that lifetime and this one." What a difficult life experience that must have been, having a strong connection to both sides in the war.

The Rolex was definitely symbolic of our love; it was his wedding 'ring' and is visible in almost every photo I have of Don (I love that). But Don said that for him it was also symbolic because he loved his roots and loved his father in his previous life. This explained why the Rolex had always felt highly emotive; it was symbolic on so many levels.

Annette asked if he had another life in Germany before that, which would explain a stronger pull to Germany. "No, he says, 'I was in Russia before that. It seems I've been around.'" Annette said he was laughing. Which made us laugh as well.

Don and Annette went on to explain about *our* previous lifetime and said, "In the last life we shared, we weren't *allowed* to be together, so this lifetime made up for that unrequited love."

This really pulled at my heart and explained the depth of our connection and the desperation we both felt when separated, for any period of time, in this life.

"Never to be torn apart," Don said. Annette wasn't sure why he was saying that but then Don went on to say, "Till death do us part, marriage vows – who ever made up those words because that's not true either." We both said, "We didn't part!" Damn, I love this man!

Then I was told I was a princess or royalty or something in our last shared life, which was why we just couldn't be together. Don said, "Tell her princesses couldn't always speak for themselves either." This was Don giving me information that was significant to me in this life. I understood he was referring to my propensity to avoid speaking up for myself in this life. Don went on to say, "I wasn't an acceptable beau," and laughed. He enjoyed the element of notoriety. Some things obviously don't change between lives.

Annette said, "This life was in Spain and is where I was the princess; however, I have had several lives in Spain." Spain is significant to me. Two lifetimes at least in Spain with Don, although it wasn't called Spain at that time. I have personally felt a strong connection to Spain and was intrigued by the history of the Spanish Armada at school. This was fascinating.

I was told that as well as being a princess, I was a dancer, a ballerina and was very talented, and I used to sing. That was my medicine; go into my own vibration through singing. I was advised that I wasn't allowed to perform because of who I was. It was devastating to me. I had to follow the rules my father made. My mother had no say whatsoever, but my sister could dance because she was underneath me, and as the eldest I was a direct line to the throne. Annette says it was horrible for me as I was the better dancer.

Then Don advised, "Back before that one, in the life we shared before the previous one, Pam was unacceptable for him and his status in the eyes of his family."

Don was showing Annette a body of water with a drawbridge to an old castle. I was told I was in that castle around 1700–1800. She wasn't sure which lifetime but thinks I was a servant in that castle, which meant Don could have been a nobleman. I was told if it wasn't England, maybe it was Scotland.

It would be funny if I had been a wench as this would provide a connection with the costume he had me wear when we had Dirty Dick's theatre restaurant. Ha-ha!

I said, "It's funny that in this life there was that unacceptable element in us being together as well because Don was twice my age when we met."

So, we had our last two lifetimes with roles reversed, where I wasn't acceptable, then he wasn't acceptable. And, in this life, there was an element of unacceptability, but *we were able to be together because we stood our ground.*

Don clapped and said, "Bravo to us."

I said, "Yes! Bravo to us!"

It was also interesting that I was a ballerina and not allowed to dance because I don't dance in this life at all! And I never understood why I had such an aversion to dancing. I referenced earlier the relevance of the 'Perfect' song, and how Don had developed a work-around to my reluctance to dancing. He would hug me and sway while humming.

We had such an intense love for each other because this life together carried so much heavy emotion caused by separation, heartache and pain, which made us inseparable in this life.

I felt one of the reasons he was telling me this was so that I would remember we were more than this lifetime. He was reminding me of this to help me with my grief, showing that our life was not limited to what I was experiencing then. To remember that our life together was eternal. This life was merely another chapter, not 'the story'. And it was all planned.

We are not the sum total of our experiences here. I know this.

I understood so much more about our relationship after this. I understood the powerful spark that was ignited when we first met and our reluctance to be separated. The culmination of emotions over *three lifetimes* made my experience of losing Don in this life unbearable.

In the reading with Rouna, three months after Don died, Don said he was so proud that I wasn't hiding the pain. But knowing the depth of emotions I carried were from three lives, there would have been no holding any of the pain from view. I was always going to be an open book on this.

I understood that this life with him was a gift that was incredibly valuable for both of us. It was always going to end, that's what happens with life here. It was always going to be devastating for me to be left behind due to our strong love, but this was further exacerbated by our desperate need to never be apart because of the effect the past lives had on this one. No wonder I felt shattered.

I knew in my heart now that this was why Don had repeatedly told me he would never leave me, and he hasn't. He knew how devastating losing him in this life/experience was going to be and promised to remain until my end here. This book was to come out of my excruciating pain. And so, it has.

In this reading, when I needed to hear more from Don, he picked up on this. Souls on the other side undoubtedly have impeccable intuition and they will know what you need from them, maybe even more than you do.

What does my head and heart know? Our existence is not limited to our life on Earth at this time. We have all had previous lives, sometimes with people we are close to now. There are some likes, dislikes, fears and connections that are not easily explained in the context of this life. I now have an even greater appreciation of the fact that I am more complex than I even know.

I have a fear of any water that is over my head and I have never learned to swim. I am sure I have drowned in a previous life. Our daughter developed a strong phobia of birds. Following a random statement about this in a reading, she was advised that she had been a witch in a previous life and was burned at the stake (not the first time she has been told this). However, she was told, while still alive, she had then been picked to death by birds. And yep that would be a good basis for an intense phobia originating in a previous life.

There are some documented cases where people, after a head injury, have started speaking a language they didn't previously know. I have always held a belief that these people are accessing a language they spoke in a previous life.

This would also explain how child prodigies can instinctively play at a level they have not had enough time to master in this lifetime. Who were they in a previous life?

So, this is why I asked in Part I, Chapter 1 for you to pause and assess any judgement you had regarding our relationship. We are conditioned to judge. And so, we do. But I hope you can see now that, our relationship, although viewed as wrong, was in fact, very right. It was meant to be.

It wasn't easy, at the age of eighteen, being in a relationship criticised by so many, but we were meant to be together and to fight against the prejudice. As a result, we were stronger as individuals and as a couple. We could not have been more committed to each other. Bravo to us!

new love 1980   *still very much in love 35 years later*

from my heart to yours...

Humanity likes to judge others but really, how can we? We have *no idea* of others' back story. I certainly don't. What is really going on? I would like to think we could all be more openminded when we judge ourselves, others and situations.

So, my story is, in part, about talking to my dead husband and learning what a massive impact past lives had on this one. A woman at the dog park told me reincarnation and communicating with the dead is the devil at work. That doesn't make sense to me on any level because this is about love. Love to the devil is probably like sunlight to Dracula. My life and yours are a testament to the magic of deep, pure love, and love is the currency that connects us to *Higher Power et al*. It's all good!

My first introduction to past lives was reading *Many Lives, Many Masters* by Brian Weiss. It was a fascinating read but not once did I think there would be anything interesting in my past. How wrong was I! This was amazing and gave me a depth of knowledge about myself I could not have received elsewhere. I recommend both the book and having a past-life reading.

I know Annette advised a woman I know to have a past life reading after her husband had been gone a couple of months. He wasn't able to communicate as easily because he was described as a young soul. Perhaps the past life will shed light on why they had the parting in this life that they did. Everything happens for a reason.

*In most cases,
the universe does not allow
us to move forward until
we have honoured
where we are right now.*

Unknown

26

Guiding me with clarity

9th August – twenty months and five days since Don left this world

Although I felt so much wiser by now, I still couldn't seem to hold any positivity in my life. I had gone back to Melanie to try to get some perspective on why it was so bad and what I needed to do. I still didn't have a job. I felt stuck. I was still between the life with Don and my solo life.

The moment we started the reading Don was there and was telling me I needed to calm down, to go with the change and accept it. I felt I wanted change, but I knew I was also scared of it. I wasn't saying no to any opportunities, I just wasn't seeing any.

Don said, "You're a great inspiration to family and friends and you don't even know it. Don't worry, just go with the flow at the moment. You have been so brave."

This was why I missed Don so much. He was always so encouraging and solid and calm. It was understandable that I was struggling because Don always provided a level of reassurance that I hadn't yet been able to give myself since he died.

He said, "There will be change when you're ready. Nothing is kicking you down the street. Your intuition is going to start taking off big time."

That was what I needed to hear because I had always intuitively known what to do, but that intuition disappeared in the grief fog. I was told I needed to be aware of what I was thinking. And to listen to my heart with everything.

Don said, "The last couple of months you have been suffering and you know now that you actually needed the time out from working." Don knew how important it was for me to hear this. I had been beating myself up because I hadn't found work, but the job didn't come because I wasn't ready.

"You're gifted and highly intelligent." (Oh bless him – my auto response is "Go on...") This made me smile because it brought up memories. Whenever Don paid me a compliment, and he did regularly, I would make a production of getting comfortable and say, "Go on." Ha-ha!

Melanie said he knew I was feeling alone and lost but that I didn't need to – Don was beside me – and she said she could see his big beaming smile. In my mind I could see it too.

I was told to accept the love and love the baby (my granddaughter). She was growing quickly. He said, "The baby adores you. She knows who you are, she knows who I am. *She knows everything.*

Our granddaughter has come in as love and blessings and Sparky has too."

I was asked if I'd heard noises in the new ensuite.

"Yes, it's like something small is dropped but I know no-one's there, so I ignore it as random house noises."

Melanie said, "Don spends time in the new bathroom. He makes the noise."

She reiterated that I had a huge connection with this man. I needed to just sit quietly and talk to him and I would hear him. She said, "Don is saying, 'We were *so devoted to each other and that emotion doesn't go anywhere, it's still here.*'" She went on to say that he was around me and supporting me and he wanted new things for me.

This was just over twenty months since Don had died. I knew I would grieve for a long time but never anticipated it would be like this. I was being told I needed to be releasing emotion through more crying. If crying was an Olympic sport, I would have won Gold! But I was told the more I cried, the easier it would be for me.

Melanie asked, "Are you returning to Thailand?"

"Yes, I'm taking our children for Don's birthday and the two-year mark to volunteer at the Elephant Nature Park in Chiang Mai. This trip also has the benefit of us all contributing to a truly humanitarian venture and will be the last family holiday ever as our children's lives take off in other directions."

She said, "Don's saying, 'And what about me? I will be there.'" I was told it was something really special we were doing, and we would feel Don's presence.

Melanie said, "You're going to buy something special over there and you'll buy it because it's from Don, and you will know it's from him but you should not go looking for it. You will know it when you see it. It may be a mother and baby elephant in a heart or something like that. But it's a gift from Don. It's all good!"

My emotions were running high, and Melanie correctly said, "You're thinking you're a good decision-maker but question whether you are making the right decisions." She said, "Yes, you are!" Whew! It is so easy for me to overthink everything and ultimately, come to an assumption that if I'm still hurting, still struggling with life that I must be making the wrong decisions. I'm being told I still am making the right decisions. Hurting and struggling at this stage is still part of my journey because the love was so deep, the connection so strong.

She said, "They have you walking over a swing bridge." (I really hate those things, but this scenario perfectly reflected how I had felt!) I had been swaying from side to side. Don said, "It's okay, we've needed to shake you up sometimes to get the emotions and crying out but it's going to straighten up for you."

They also said that I needed to let my vibrations/emotions go low (deep depression, feelings of hopelessness) because this was how I would let the grief and crying out. "When you need to cry, cry. Know that Don is with you. Know that everything is going to be okay. Your mind is so active you need to engage it in something like walking or painting."

Don said, "I know you are going to be okay. I can see a lot clearer from over here what is going on."

This statement was significant to me because I trusted him more than I trusted myself at that moment; he only ever wanted what was good for me and he could see what was happening. This gave me greater assurance that everything would be fine.

I was told, *"Know and believe that there is more going on than we can see down here.* Don is manifesting and he's helping you manifest what you want, and it will come through."

I was also told there was something for me to release in NZ and the new job couldn't have happened before the trip to NZ. I wasn't looking forward to the trip 'home' and it was coming up so quickly. I would be there in five days. It's where our families still lived and where we had so much history because it's where we met and lived for half of our life together. I was worried about how I would be able to manage my emotions given they were already off the charts!

Melanie said, "NZ will be a bit daunting but know that Don is with you. This is part of what you both need to do to settle that aspect of your lives here. NZ will be okay. You will be in and out. Talk to him in your head, that's where it's at now."

I said I was afraid because I'd been through so much deep sadness, grief and disappointment. Melanie said Archangel Michael was supporting me. "Spirit is saying, *'We know what we are doing. Trust us.'* They say, 'At this time, loneliness is your biggest problem.'"

"Yes, I would agree with that!"

Melanie went on to say that I was going to be here for a long time yet but when the doors open (when I die), Don would be there and what a wonderful reunion that would be!

Don told me, "You're going to do a lot of travelling, new opportunities, new ways of looking at life. You need to be commended because you have done so well through everything and that was my biggest fear of ever leaving you. *But you will be speaking your truth on everything.* Don't worry."

Melanie turned over a couple of cards, so I wouldn't see them, but I did. They were about love coming into my life. I called her on it, and she said, "You may not be ready to hear this."

I told her, "It's been said in every other reading (with others) and I've rejected the idea every time. Previously, I didn't want to hear it and have declared it's never going to happen. But I know it's time for me to 'go with the flow', as Don said, and I'm tired of feeling like I'm pushing against life. It's not so much that I'm accepting this, more like I no longer have the energy to reject anything."

They told me there was a new love but not yet. When I was ready for it, it would happen. Melanie said I could say to spirits one day I was ready for a friend to have coffee with and have conversations with. Then this man would enter my life.

I had a *deja vu* moment and a clearer understanding of how life works! Before I met Don, I had rejected every request for a date I received. I wasn't ready for a relationship. One day I decided to change my auto response. A cute guy who I'd rejected several times and who still wanted a relationship with me, was asking again. This time I was more prepared to say yes. But that night I met Don, and without any knowing intention of hooking up with Don, I said no (again) to the other guy. The next day I accepted an unexpected dinner invitation from Don.

I met Don when I said to myself (universe) I was ready for a relationship. Don was 'the one'. So, I understand the poetic synchronicity of life and that the most unexpected but right person showed up the last time I put it out there and will again when I say I am ready.

So, although I wasn't ready, I now accepted this would happen, but what was harder to digest was having this conversation, which I never expected to ever have, with Don. I had decided after Don died there would never be another relationship, and I was happy for Don to be my *only* relationship in this life, because we lived a true love story.

But *Don* was telling me there would be another man coming. That was just incomprehensible. Melanie went on to say, "Don is marking territory. He's saying, 'Not good enough,' 'Not good enough,' 'Yeah, he's okay.'" He was actually reviewing candidates for the man that would enter my life. This was unreal – that he could see what was coming and guide the circumstances. I really just wanted him, but that wasn't going to happen. This was unbelievable.

Side note: In writing this book, I have the benefit of revisiting the conversation with Don seventeen months earlier. In that reading he tried to gently advise me there would be another relationship. He had said the following after I totally rejected the idea, but I understand this better now:

*"If someone else comes into your life, you don't want it to be like us because you learned what love is and you learned because we had the best relationship. And with anyone else it doesn't matter **because it's just going to be a relationship.** You don't need to learn the lesson about **what love is** because you have had the best, because we had the best together, it's not me, it's what **we had** that was the best."*

I already have relationships with other people; I have friends and none of them are anything like my relationship with Don, but they are still in my life. Of course, I could do this. It was never going to be about replacing Don.

Melanie said, "You will allow this new person to come into your life. You have learned a hell of a lot in this life and now you have to trust yourself."

I can tell you now though, it took me a long time to fully accept this was in my future and that Don was orchestrating it. It felt like I'd woken up in the middle of a damn soap opera.

Another understanding I have about 'life' now is that the relationship Don and I had in this life, healed the pain of separation and unrequited love we both carried because we were kept apart in our *last two lives together*. Don's story/life ended with giving and receiving unconditional love with me.

My story is ongoing, and although I have some healing from the past lives by living in unconditional love with Don, I now carry in my soul the pain of separation and a broken heart in this life. Argh!

So, I was told the new man was coming in to *heal* my heart and I would be doing that for him as well. He had suffered as I had, and he would understand. He wouldn't suffocate me.

Don was laughing and saying, "You are in for a big surprise."

Melanie said, "Wouldn't it be funny if he's got a similar name as Don."

I had an inkling of what would be 'funny' in our eyes but it's another one of those private jokes that will remain between us. Only time would tell what he was referring to in that statement.

Melanie went on to say, "You haven't fully accepted Don has gone home." Dammit, I thought I had, isn't that why I cry so much! She said, "You need to trust in your own integrity and know that your guides have got you where you are. Don't put pressure on yourself as you have this feeling that you are holding everything up (job and finances); it's because you aren't done with grieving Don yet."

Melanie said, "You've been in major shock. Massive. It's an acceptance thing and you'll accept when you're ready. You will know when you're ready. You know when you want a cup of tea, don't you? It's the same. Don't listen to others about your grief."

In the same reading seventeen months earlier, I remember Don telling me, "It's about the heart, it's got nothing to do with time." Really, twenty-one months is a short amount of time when we shared thirty-seven years (and two previous unrequited love lives together). But it felt like I had been carrying this pain forever already!

The concept of acceptance had been cropping up a lot. The technique for acceptance seemed silly (refer to the Survival Toolkit, Part III), but I would try anything now. I wanted to 'live' with my loss, not merely exist in what was left of this life.

So, I understood when Melanie said it was an acceptance thing.

I also had to review my habit of blaming myself for things not happening as I expected. Knowing that the swinging emotions were not my failing but the spirits helping me heal, helped me accept that there was more going on than I could comprehend. And that I needed to trust that everything was happening for a reason and it wasn't *wrong*.

Also, the job hadn't come because it wasn't the right time for me; I had more healing to do first.

These messages were important to me. *"Spirits were saying, 'We know what we are doing. Trust us.'"* And Don was saying, *"I know you are going to be okay. You can see a lot clearer from over here what is going on."*

from my heart to yours…

I believe what we need to know is repeatedly put in front of us until we pay attention. I kept seeing or hearing the word acceptance. Then Melanie mentioned it, and then a technique for acceptance randomly came to my attention. Message received. Time to take action.

Then there were the messages in my head. Do you ever have a lyric from a song just repeatedly pop into your head? If so, listen and take notice. I heard Imagine Dragons' 'Trust me darling' in my head, and I knew they were put there by Don. And I did trust him, I always had. That hadn't changed.

What messages are you receiving? Messages are not just sent via feathers and songs; the thoughts that are niggling you are messages as well. Take notice. They are sending you help and guidance from the other side.

I've already been told that Don knows what is going on, and that he can see more than I can. Your loved one is in this same situation; even without Don's help, my guides are there guiding us all with a clarity we don't have here.

There is this premise, during grieving, that you get to a point where 'you move on', 'you get over it'. This was an after-death requirement I struggled with because it seemed impossible. I wasn't even sure I wanted to get to that place, but I didn't want to suffer indefinitely either. Therefore, Don's words made total sense when he said, "We were so devoted to each other and that emotion doesn't go anywhere, it's still here."

The love you feel for someone doesn't fade with time, and that's okay. You will find ways of coping with life without letting go of the love that connected you. It really isn't going anywhere. Love doesn't die.

Don also said I would be 'speaking my truth' on everything. It made writing this book so much easier. To start with, I tried to filter everything so as not to make others uncomfortable (much like other books I had read about death). But I realised grief is uncomfortable and to try to hide this was counterproductive and was further perpetrating the premise that we must hide strong emotion. That is not the message I want you to receive.

If you feel deep emotions, that's more than okay. What's not okay is people not letting you have a voice during a period where you need to be able to be open and honest about how you are. There is an 'R U OK' day, but what we need to realise is that there are 365 'R U OK' days in a year. Don and I never celebrated Valentine's Day because, we said, "You have shown me love and respect for 364 days, then you are off the hook on February 14."

Yesterday is history, tomorrow is a mystery, but today is a gift, that is why it's called the present.

Bil Keane

27
"Really, it's been two years already!"
4th December – twenty-four months since Don left this world

It felt surreal to recognise the passing of two years. So much and so little had changed in that time. At the beginning it was impossible to comprehend that I could be at this place in time. Every day crawled by. But I got there. Don was still by my side and I had a level of acceptance that supported me, even though I still missed and loved him intensely.

I created an anniversary video for the second wedding anniversary we *didn't have*. I wanted to share this with family and friends on Facebook, knowing it would reappear every anniversary. It was a great tribute to Don and our relationship, and, after publishing it, I could watch it whenever I wanted to. Two different people, with experience in media, had been engaged to do this for me but it didn't happen, or it wasn't right. In the end I did it myself. I worked it out because this was a job *I* was to do. And so it was.

Don, the protector of my state of mind, sometimes interfered when I watched the video if I was too emotional. One time when I was watching it, the tears were streaming down my face and it just cut out. He was saying, '*Stop!*' Another time, it stopped just after I quoted Don as saying, "Love you, Pam." But most of the time, I watched it and appreciated the gift this person was in my life, and it played without interruption.

One of the highlights in these two years was volunteering at the Elephant Nature Park, ten months after Don died. Although devastated at the time, I knew I had to prove to myself I could have an interesting and rewarding life, *if I just put some effort into it.* The park gave me the chance to focus on giving, when I was consumed by what had been taken from me.

It was an incredible experience and, as promised, I returned the following year with our children to mark the anniversary of their father's death and his birthday. We went to the park to celebrate his life amongst these wonderful creatures who were now in a new place, like Don, free of fear and pain.

Death had given me a new perspective on living, so for our children:

- ♡ I wanted them to get a fresh perspective on what was important in life. In today's world, life dramas tend to make meaningless stuff seem important and so we miss the important stuff, like making your piece in this world a better place through love and respect for self and others.

- ♡ I wanted them to see Don's tree, planted in his honour and with his ashes. A gift I was given by people who had never met Don but cared anyway.

- ♡ I wanted them to experience true humanitarian work and caring on a whole new level where giving without any expectation of receiving was the culture.

- ♡ In one of the most caring environments on Earth, I wanted them to remember their father for his greatest contribution to humanity. He made the world a better place because he loved and cared for everyone he met and was deeply loved in return.

"Really, it's been two years already!"

Harley, Stacey and I with Lek, the founder of the Elephant Nature Park and the most amazingly compassionate person I have every met.

It was an incredibly special shared experience where we met some wonderful people from around the world, shovelled more elephant poop and kept the cycle going by feeding them as well. We had our photo taken with the tree (that Fa Mai, a mischievous ten-year-old elephant had tried to uproot and eat), had a birthday cake for Don organised by Karin, a fellow volunteer, and our guides Guy, Waroom and Joke. We also shared the cake with our new friends from Canada, Tanya and Kim. From Tanya I learned you can have ashes added to tattoo ink so I may one day add colour, with Don's ashes in it, to the angel wings on my tattoo.

My daughter had an incredible experience with a blind elephant called Jokia (translates to Eye from Heaven) and she vowed to return to experience it again on her own. The elephant approached her and just rested her trunk beside Stacey. This trip was life changing for her. It made her feel she could be who she was and gave her a depth of strength she didn't know she had. I made a commitment to myself to return every year. Well-intentioned plans made before COVID-19 said, *'STOP!'*

Stacey and Jokia, having a moment

from my heart to yours...

Life isn't supposed to be an endless holiday. Mishaps are normal. I have challenges in my life now that I didn't expect to have, but that's life and I have a good life because I refuse to see it any other way. Life is about our choices, our attitude and our gratitude for what we have and an appreciation for today, living in the present moment.

I absolutely avoid any thoughts of regrets. I appreciate the gift Don gave me by dying when he did. He released himself from this life so that he never had to live 'as a burden' (his words). He is free now. And for me he gave me freedom which I had never experienced before. It is not that I am better off without him, it is merely that this is my life and I will live it as much as possible with a positive attitude. I have freedom and I still have Don, just in a different form. He still continues to love and support me in everything, and he is perfect!

I didn't have the money when I decided to go to the Elephant Park either time, but it happened anyway. And the park gave me the chance to focus on giving, when I was consumed by what had been taken from me. I have used this technique before. When you are down, if you do something unconditionally for someone else, it is a real mood changer. The park took this to a whole new level. I really couldn't imagine what the last two years would have been like without this experience. It jump-started my healing. The amount of determination and strength I had to call on to get there created something special and an understanding that my life was up to me. I did it!

a different family photo with Don posing as a tree

Death makes you appreciate life, and after you get over the feeling you have lost control, you realise you always had control. What you lost was enthusiasm for life and it is exhilarating when you take it back with a vengeance.

Yesterday I was clever, so I wanted to change the world. Today I am wise, so I am changing myself.

Rumi

28

I'm not done yet, there's more...

I still receive music, butterflies, feathers and birds, but only periodically now. I know Don is with me all the time and at times I feel his presence, so I don't need the messages as much as I used to.

I have also felt his presence *in me* on occasion. I had thought the energy healing session where Don transfused my body with pure love had been a 'once-in-a-lifetime experience', but I have experienced Don's energy in me and around me to varying degrees since.

Whenever I hear words in my head that make me cry, I know these are Don's words. It's not like hearing a sentence coming together as each word is said, instead it's like the whole sentence/dialogue is instantly downloaded and in your head.

Then, while I was in NZ, I experienced something that was both uplifting and heartbreaking at the same time.

I had gone to my father's walking group, which consists of people with breathing and/or mobility difficulties, and they slowly make their way around a circuit inside a hall, recording laps and time taken. My father has emphysema. He enjoys the social aspects of being part of this group where they enjoy a cuppa and cake and the friendships he and Mum have made there.

While sitting and watching, I felt, very strongly, Don's anguish in my body. He was saying, *'This is what I didn't want for myself and why I had to go when I did.'* I struggled to keep myself from crying while I was sitting there. I could feel his pain as if it were my own. The feeling was intense. This was his greatest fear and I felt his agony strongly at this time. I can only ever feel honoured when he shares on that level with me. Every day, I share with him the anguish his death has caused me. But that's okay. We're good. We're still a team.

Don had told me I would feel his energy in the music and in things he put in front of me and that I would know it was him. I didn't understand this for a while but once I realised that when I felt connected to a song or something, it was Don's energy, and I knew in my heart I couldn't be any closer to him than we were now.

One of the ways they can communicate is through moving pictures on the wall. My daughter and I have both experienced pictures tilting or falling off the wall. We would ring each other and discuss what it meant based on which picture had fallen. I didn't fully appreciate this until I was babysitting my granddaughter one night when she was six months old.

Melanie had told me our granddaughter knew who I was and who Don was and that she knew everything. There is an understanding that babies and infants remember where they have come from (and more) but lose this knowledge either with time or because of societal pressures.

All I know is that at my home, she *always* stares and laughs at two photos of Don on the photo wall. She also used to look past my shoulder when I was holding her, and I knew she was smiling at Don. It's where he would have been standing in life and this tells me he's in the same place in sprit as well. It was also the same as when Sparky barked at the empty landing; I *knew* he was seeing Don.

I'm not done yet, there's more…

On one particular occasion, while my granddaughter was with me and I was struggling with my emotions, she put her hand out to a different family photo taken when *her* dad was two years old. She started laughing. I asked her whether she was laughing at her dad or Poppa (Don).

The photo Lilly pointed to that then fell off the wall was the small pink one on the bottom right side

I took her upstairs to bed feeling that I was ill-equipped to care for her when I felt so inadequate in my own life. While upstairs I heard a thump downstairs. When I came down, the photo she had laughed at had fallen off the wall. I said aloud, "What's the message?" It came into my head later. They were saying, *'You've got this. Remember when you had babies and you loved them, and it was just natural to know what to do.'*

Yes, I was beating myself up when I had all the skills and knowledge and love in me that I needed to care for my precious granddaughter.

My six-month-old granddaughter pointed this out to me, and I didn't get the message, so spirit knocked the picture off the wall so I would pay attention. Don't worry, I know how crazy this sounds if you are new to this. Remember that at one point I had no idea this could happen either.

My own daughter, who is open to receiving messages, has had interesting experiences as well. Her father-in-law, Michael, died three months before her dad. She has a photo and candle for each under the TV. On occasion, when I've been there for dinner, I've seen Don's candle flame dance much higher than Michael's. It was more evident that Don was using his to let us know he was there because the candles were side by side and exposed to identical air currents. There was no discernible scientific explanation for the difference.

Originally, I had been told I would sell the house six months after Don died. I didn't. It took me two years to get myself mentally prepared and motivated to do this; it just felt too hard for so long. When I did sell, everything happened quickly. Settlement was twenty-four days, and I had to find my own place for the first time in my life. After being unemployed for ten months, I was offered a job the day before I moved, with an immediate start. It all happened so quickly I had little time to dwell on the fact that I was letting go of the physical environment we had shared. It also meant I didn't have time to push against what was happening.

Six months after Don died, he told me through Melanie that he was sweeping the path in front of me, making sure all opportunities were ready when I was. I had no doubt Don guided the house sale and he also led me to my next place. I was sure he, and my guides, made it happen so quickly I didn't have time to rethink and just had to go with the flow, because he knew me.

The moment I viewed the unit, I knew this was it for me, but after a week in my new home, it hit me; I was sitting in the room I visualised sitting in, multiple times with Don in the 'Coping with Grief' meditation by Jason Stephenson almost two years earlier. I looked out of the big window I had clearly seen in the meditation and said to Don, "I can see your hand in this, thank you, it's perfect."

Don knew I would love it. I could see him smiling at me. I understood what he and my guides were doing in my life then. It was all good!

Twenty-eight months after Don died, I am okay publicly but naturally still have periods of deep sadness and loneliness and feeling tired of the dips in my emotional state. It's one thing to impose self-isolation on yourself; it's another when it is forced on you by COVID-19.

I was recently feeling extremely lonely. I felt I had done all I could, so it was time to get someone to help me. Both Stacey and Melanie had recently seen Cara, an Emotion and Body Code energy healer who lifts stuck emotions that we accumulate from our life experiences. I'd never heard of this before, but they were enthusiastic about the treatment they had received so I would give it a try. I wanted to try something new because parts of the grieving just felt stuck, so I thought I'd give that a go.

Cara told me what (stuck emotions) were holding me where I was. Her job was to lift them, essentially releasing me from emotions and energy that were not serving me and making life hard/er.

Interestingly but not surprisingly, of the sixteen cords of emotional energy identified, fourteen of them were attached to Don's death. They included feelings of abandonment, crying, anger, longing (came up twice), overwhelmed, shock, frustration, grief, anxiety, despair, fearfulness, nervousness, worry and physical emotional shock energy. The word longing was very emotional for me. I felt that one deeply. The session was a phone call; I did nothing but felt lighter afterwards. Cara also gave me insight on the 'insurance' money Don had repeatedly referenced. It predated when we met, and I would not have known about it without guidance from the other side.

For so long I felt grounded and this tale resonated. There is a parable about an eagle's egg that is found and placed in the chicken coup. The eagle is raised by chickens and never realises his capacity to soar even though he has everything he needs to do so. The eagle died, never knowing what it felt like to soar. I cried when I heard this story and have found I'm more sensitive to some situations because they resonate with my pain.

I had forgotten what it was like to be free, even though I had everything I needed to fly. What had I lost in grieving? What was missing? *Self-appreciation, self-love.*

In grief, I had convinced myself the life I had lived held value *only* because of Don; the laughter in my life was only there *because* of Don. Of course, this wasn't correct; he reflected back what I put out and vice versa.

I will always miss sharing a laugh with Don, but I can and will laugh again. The value part is harder because we did some amazing things, and during the unexpected bumps, we had one constant: each other. Now I face bumps in life without that ballast. But I feel whole again. As an individual, I have everything I need to succeed.

I understand more about living now and pay more attention to his advice than I did when he was here (eyeroll). He's holding my life's blueprint, after all. He knows what's important. Recently, he told me to 'stop tiring myself over things I had no control over'. So, when I find myself doing exactly this, I stop! It seems easier to control myself because I am infinitely wiser than the day my life turned to a pile of excrement.

Don was an amazing person, whose light was dimming with age. Now, present-day Don, although not physically here, is back to his vibrant, capable self. I am now more accepting of his current form because I have experiences, since he died, that are priceless. This is the Don I know is beside me. It is the same as loving someone at twenty, and although they are different at fifty you still love them. You accept the change. Don is still Don. Although he is different, he is still recognisable as Don, and I love him deeply. What we have *now* is more perfect than the learning experience we shared together and called life. I could not have loved Don more in life; in death that love has a pureness because no earthly dramas can touch it.

from my heart to yours...

I explained at the start of this book that I suffered three losses when Don died. I imagine this could be the same for everyone. Is there such a thing as good grief? In reality, it is this:

 The loved one: Good grief is knowing you contributed in a positive way to this person's life and they ultimately went home *feeling deeply loved*. Only love is real. Only love survives.

 Us: Good grief is knowing you have shared love – be it with a partner, relative, friend or pet – that is *so pure it survives death*. Grief is love. Love doesn't die.

You: Good grief is knowing that you experienced the worst life can throw at you *only* because you experienced the best there is in life – pure unconditional love. You *will* survive from horrendous grief and you *will* eventually be stronger.

Don's death put my life in perspective. Although he was *my* partner, I know 'soulmates' can be anyone, and I truly believe we are not limited to one soulmate. Because we are only looking for a specific 'one', and assuming it is a spouse, we probably miss the significance of others in our life.

I believe the people we connect more deeply with here are from our *soul family or soul tribe*. For you, deep love may be held by a partner, child, grandchild, dear friend, parent, grandparent or even a pet. Love knows no bounds. Whether they are still walking this Earth or have passed, treasure it! Being held in someone else's heart in a space of deep, unconditional love is the ultimate prize in life. Not everyone gets that! Some think it is about money (eyeroll).

For it was not into my ear you whispered but into my heart. It was not my lips you kissed, but my soul.

Unknown

29
How does this story end?
Over four years since Don left this world

*D*on came, he experienced wonderful blessings and heartbreaking lessons, then he went home. His life here was complete. However, his presence and influence in mine and our children's and others' lives will continue to be felt until we, too, have gone. At the conclusion of my life, I will be reunited with Don. Without cutting myself short, I am really looking forward to the reunion. I have so much to thank him for when I see him, and I owe him a thump on the arm for what he has put me through.

In the meantime, he will be beside me every step of my life.

To him, no 'time' will have passed by the time I die. To me, I will have lived another twenty to thirty or so years. But one thing I know is that regardless of time, the woman *I am here* will love the man *he was here,* until I die, and my soul already loves him unconditionally for eternity. Such is life.

This life is merely a chapter. Don played his part in my life superbly and now he is in the wings cheering me on. Our loved ones don't leave us, of this I am sure.

Love doesn't die and relationships don't end because a body died. Don will forever be a part of my life because he's with me, he's in my heart and connected to me at soul level. He was the placeholder for thirty-seven years of incredible memories, where he stood beside me while I became the strong person I was before he died.

Since then he has stood beside me during my *grieving, healing and restructuring*. The post-death memories I now have are the most perfect expressions of pure love and are from the other side.

I don't remember every time Don gave me flowers while he was alive, but I will always remember the feather he floated on the wind to place in my hand.

I miss sitting across from him in a restaurant or café, but it warms my heart remembering entering restaurants 'without him' to find he is playing 'our song'.

He made me laugh so easily throughout our life, but the comedic bird is an encore I never expected, and it is exceptional.

When I'm having coffee and a gentle breeze lifts the hair from my neck – that's him.

When a feather lays on my path, he's left me a gift.

When a voice in my head is urging me to greater things, that's him encouraging me.

Losing Don was massive. It was heartbreaking on a whole new level. I have always *loathed* the term 'unrequited love', and now I know why. I suffered it twice already with this soul, and this time makes three!.

When we met in this lifetime, our souls connected and manifested a space of unexplained and absolute calm with each other, which continued for thirty-seven years. Life was not perfect, but our relationship only grew stronger through every adversity. Together we were greater than the parts.

True suffering comes from loving deeply and remaining behind, shattered. Throughout my grieving I was looking for peace. Knowing our love for each other continues gives me a sense of peace and the gift of eternity. Because this is not over. Love doesn't die.

I look at Sparky and my granddaughter and say to them "I love you. Thank you for coming into my life." How wonderful it is now to appreciate the gift that some people and animals are in my life.

My life continues with an appreciation of time and timing that I didn't have before. Life flows in sync with *when you are ready for the next step*, so I don't stress on timing now. Since Don died, I lost the winder for his Rolex, which was also his wedding ring. I was devastated but later came to understand he was telling me time is not relevant. Our love is eternal. Our big clock on the wall is only right twice a day. That is deliberate. It is a daily reminder that the *passage and measurement* of time is irrelevant, no matter what the clock says, you only have right now.

Don is very much still in my thoughts and in my heart. I still cry but sometimes feel it is more in wonder of the intense love we continue to share and deep gratitude for the incredible life we had. Other times, I feel I am being propelled to release lingering feelings of grief and sadness to make way for new life and love. My granddaughters have shown me how deeply I can love again.

The new guy, previously predicted, is not in my life yet; he won't come until I am ready. Most importantly, I know I am being given time for me, to be on my own, and gain a deep understanding of who I am, now. Only after this, will I invite someone into my life. I will not look for him, I am happy to let it be on divine timing and know he will just appear when the time is right. I'm not in a hurry. No one will ever replace Don. I know this. Our love is eternal.

Part III:
Survival toolkit – self-care in progress

You cannot stop
the birds of sorrow
from flying over your head,
but you can stop them
nesting in your hair.

Unknown

Every healer or healing recommended to me, I took and gave it a try. I was constantly looking for answers to the questions: 'How do I survive this?' and 'What will give me some peace?'

In the process of trying everything, I found there is no cure for grief. There are no short cuts. Grief is love. You can't *decide* to love someone less. If you are suffering intense grief, then I say that's wonderful; painful but wonderful. It's a reflection of deep love.

If I did this over again, knowing what I know now, would I change anything? In my grieving, no, the outcome would have been the same. I accept that because I love Don deeply, I will suffer deeply.

Would I have loved him less to ease the burden of losing him? Not possible. True love, pure love, unconditional love does not sit in the conscious mind. It's far deeper than that. It is what it is, so we just have to deal with it and never lose sight of the fact that loving intensely is a gift not everyone receives in this life.

I would not trade a moment of my grief for a life less loved.

So much can be learned in hindsight, but there is nothing I could have changed except to stop *wanting* the unrealistic timeframes and false expectations set by others and myself, to be real. Once I reconciled myself to missing Don *for the rest of my life,* I was released from time-centred expectations, and Don's posthumous statement helped:

"Grief, it's about the heart, it's got nothing to do with time."

Don Eade, 2018
1943–2017

Hindsight has, however, given me a new perspective on how life flows and how much I got in the way of *the flow*. If I had listened, and trusted the messages about selling our home, my life would have been easier. I thought I was on my own but when I did eventually sell, I saw how perfectly orchestrated it was. When I just let it happen, it flowed seamlessly until all of a sudden it was behind me and it had come together so easily.

I also have an appreciation on how dangerous it is to bank on your future. We made so many decisions based on the premise that there was always going to be more time. We really do only have the present moment.

But hindsight and reflecting comes later. What about now? Simply breathing will ensure your survival, but how can you make this process easier for yourself? This is a period of intense self-care.

This is my self-care survival toolkit.

> *You yourself,
> as much as anybody
> in the entire universe,
> deserve your love
> and affection.*
>
> — Buddha

30
Self-care – where do I start?

*B*elow is the list of treatments and techniques I used, and they helped me in several ways.

The list is not exhaustive. I believe anyone that uses it will be able to add to it, thereby making it attuned to the individual and a more useful list that can be handed to the next person they see who needs to invest in self-care while surviving one of life's challenges, be it loss of life, health or relationship.

At the beginning, while in a perpetual state of numbness, I just wanted to *feel* something emotionally, while at the same time the reiki sessions helped me feel less physical pain. Initially, it was a feeling of control I got from booking a massage or something that came first, then gradually I could feel something akin to relief, relaxation or peace.

Then there is the undeniable fact that chronic stress negatively affects your health. My mind and body were traumatised by my loss, so later I listened to my body to see what needed attention. I didn't want to deal with health issues on top of the grief, so I did what I could to counter the effects of chronic stress. I was actually petrified of having to deal with 'anything else' so I took preventative measures where possible.

The list is everything I consider noteworthy. When I got to a point where I had no money, I focused on the no-cost things I could do. I think it is important to note that some options appeared more effective than others, but who am I to say the ones where I didn't feel I was taking a step forward may have in fact stopped me from taking a step backwards?

I also deliberately looked at my self-care in terms of what I could do on my own and what required intervention and for me to say, "I need help."

Grief made me feel I had no control over my life – I felt powerless – so booking a treatment or being disciplined in some of my self-care enabled me to feel I had an element of power and control. I choose to believe there is some value in everything you do. It is important to understand that you never *lose* control. It is your life, and you may not act as you did previously, but the choice to act or not, you still have control over.

from my heart to yours...

I consciously avoided filling my recovery with a big 'I need help' self-care section, when there was so much self-care I needed to focus on giving myself. You can't expect others to do for you what you are not prepared to do for yourself. I felt I wasn't getting my own message if I started to rely too heavily on others for my self-care.

The order of my list is not based on importance because this changed as circumstances changed. It's alphabetical and up to you to rate their relevance to you as required.

Being able to compile a list like this can give you a sense of control. Nothing will change the grief, but by deliberately engaging in self-care, you are doing things that make you 'feel' at the least and make you feel better at the best.

I suffered for a long time feeling that I had no control over life. But this was just a feeling, I was still the boss of me. So, I set out to *feel* in control of small things and worked my way to bigger things.

Don't feel you need to do everything, or anything, based on what I did. It is 100 percent your choice as to what you do. The point is you have choices, always. *From my heart to yours.* I have shared my story and my self-care toolkit, but everyone's journey is so deeply personal and yours is entirely up to you.

I have left space below so you can add your own self-care list and hopefully experience a sense of control.

With much love,

Pam

'It's up to me' self-care

Note: This list is alphabetical, you rate each item's importance to you.

Acceptance

The advice I was given regarding acceptance was as follows:

"When you feel an emotion, accept it, acknowledge it, view it from outside yourself, do not engage in it."

The words didn't make sense to me at first, but when I tried it, I understood. When grief started to flood me, I would say to myself, in monotone as if I was observing it, 'Yes, I feel it.' And do you know what started to happen? Most of the time it dissolved; it didn't grow and consume me. I didn't start this one until about eighteen months after Don died. I don't know how easy this would have been early on.

♡ Deep breathing

Deep breathing is one of the easiest ways to reduce stress in the body. This is because when you breathe deeply, it sends a message to your brain to calm down and relax.

The first thing that happens under stress is that our breathing becomes shallow. This deprives our body and brain of the benefits of rich oxygenated blood. It reduces our 'life force energy' when we really need it and also decreases the amount of oxygen to the brain, which is essential for mental health. No wonder I was foggy!

When I found out that my breathing was contributing to my grief and discomfort, I tried to take deep breaths and found it was painful. This is not a reason to stop deep breathing, it's an indication you really need to do this.

I was advised to deep breathe for fifteen minutes every morning (I was slack on this bit) and to take ten deep breaths every time I thought about it. So, I put a little sign on my computer monitor that just said *'Breathe'*, and I would take a deep breath every time I saw it.

I understand that a longer breath out than the breath in will help you relax and is what I do as part of my getting to sleep ritual, or immediately when I get stressed and as many times as I remember during the day.

There is countless research 'out there' that tells us about the benefits of deep breathing. It slows our heart rate, oxygenates the blood and sends a 'feel good' message to the brain. This message comes from endorphins that are tiny neurochemicals released by our body.

Interestingly, I have discovered that the word endorphin comes from 'endogenous', meaning it's produced within the body, and 'morphine', which is synonymous with pain relief. In effect, endorphins are a natural pain reliever you can manufacture yourself. Breathe in, breathe out.

Candles and crystals

My daughter makes candles and made me one that was my connection to Don. I chose a relaxing fragrance and the jar. She put the following quote on the side of the jar: *"Those we love don't go away; they walk beside us every day."* I had the jar refilled regularly and three crystals, which I chose for love and peace, were added before it set.

Every night when I go to bed, I light the candle and blow it out before turning off the light. The candle has been refilled multiple times. It is Don's candle and sits beside his photo on my bedside table. It is a ritual that brings me comfort when I go to bed.

If you don't know a candle maker, find wax distributors and they will be able to tell you who is making candles as a small business/hobby. The benefit of the hobbyist is that they can provide better value and a customised candle. Commercially made candles I have found give me the same peace when I light them for Don. It was just special having one at the beginning that was his.

Choose your words

I find it easier to say, 'Don's death', but choke up when I say, 'My husband died' or 'When your father died'. 'Don's death' is about *him*; he was done, and I know he is in a good place. The other statements are about *our* loss, which is too painful and never-ending. At times, I say, "My husband died." out loud to gauge my level of healing. Work out what your trigger words are so you can avoid using them in others' company, and then use them when you are alone to help release pent-up emotions.

 **His clothes**

In the photo on my bedside table, Don is wearing a navy and tan hoodie. When I need extra comfort, I wear it and it feels like I am in a hug with him. In one of the readings I asked Don what he was wearing so I could more easily visualise him (and because I thought it was funny to say it). He described the navy and tan hoodie. Was he wearing this because it provided me comfort, or did it provide comfort because he was also wearing it? We are all connected.

My pillow has worn one of Don's t-shirts since he died. Don was a master hugger, and I missed being in a hug with my face on his chest where I could also hear/feel his heart beating. This was the closest I could get to that feeling. The feel of the fabric on my face is comforting and especially beneficial in going to sleep. Sleep is incredibly important.

I retained Don's hoodie, a dress shirt and the t-shirt (on my pillow) but now regret giving away the majority of his clothes as I have discovered I could have had a cushion or patchwork quilt made from his clothes. A friend who read a draft of this book latched onto this one and immediately organised for her husband's golf shirts to be made into a quilt for her.

 **Crying**

Holding back emotions leads to heightened stress in the body. Don't avoid things that make you cry; deliberately engage in them, especially when alone so you can release the emotions.

Self-care – where do I start?

"Tears are 1% water and 99% feelings."

Unknown

"Scientific studies have shown the act of crying is more effective than laughing or sleeping in reducing stress and also that emotional release can elevate moods better than any antidepressant." (Source: 'Why you should start crying today', *Forbes* article by Danielle Brooker.)

It is my belief that taking pills so that you don't cry/grieve is only pushing the crying and release of emotions into your future, essentially prolonging the process in the same way as taking pills to stay awake does not replace sleep, it just delays it.

 **Essential oils**

There are many ways to use essential oils. I have a relaxing blend in Don's candle and light it at bedtime. But one method I find particularly effective is a drop of lavender oil rubbed on the soles of my feet when I go to bed. You don't need to be grieving for this one to be beneficial, I have done it for years and now also do it with my grandchildren. It's good in promoting restful sleep.

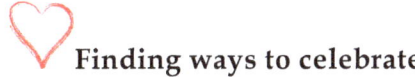 **Finding ways to celebrate**

Celebrating Don's presence in our lives created new projects that gave us so much pleasure.

Ironically, distributing Don's ashes became part of that celebration process. So far, he is in three countries, with some of his ashes sprinkled from a boardwalk on the Gold Coast of Australia, added to his parents' grave in NZ, released by our daughter on her first skydive in Australia and placed under a meditation tree sampling at the Elephant Nature Park in Thailand. And we're not done yet! COVID-19 stopped me attending a wedding in Fiji, which is another destination where I will one day sprinkle his ashes. Don worked in Fiji for a short period of time and loved it there. I will also sprinkle some ashes where Don rode speedway at Clemont Speedway in Perth.

For the family dinner on Don's birthday the year after he died, we each created an alphabetical list of unique experiences where Don had touched each of our lives. It was such a positive and heart-warmingly hilarious celebration of a wonderful and unique person.

Stacey posted a photo of Don doing one of his crazy things on Facebook and got the reaction 'keep them coming'. She committed to posting a new photo on a regular basis so we could all enjoy memories of the wonderful life we shared with him.

The anniversary video I created to celebrate our life together gave me so much pleasure, reliving wonderful times while compiling a photo montage of priceless memories that will reappear on my FB feed on our wedding anniversary every year.

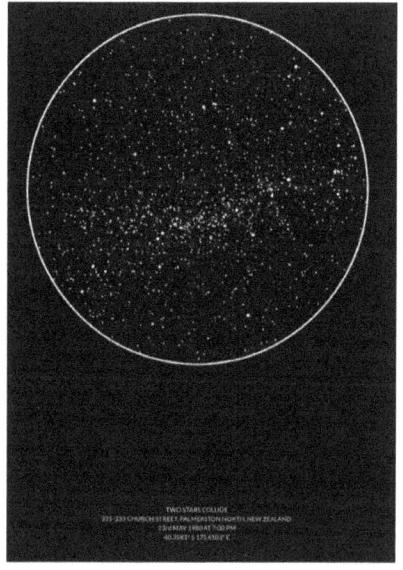

The night sky on the cover and throughout the book is the actual night sky for when and where Don and I meet. That exact time in my life when the stars aligned, and I met my future. A FaceBook post recently asked "what would you tell your 18 year old self?' My response was 'It's going to be amazing'.

That moment in time for me is so incredibly precious. Harley has his night sky for the place, date and time he married his wife. It is easy to do and very affordable. www.create.the nightsky.com

And this book.

Fresh flowers

Don asked me to buy flowers from him and Ernest and to know that they were from them. It is a precious reminder I am loved and is uplifting every time I look at them.

There are multiple references as to the therapeutic value of having fresh flowers in the home, and it's not only that they look fresh, they actually freshen the air, help improve people's mood and maintain a relaxed atmosphere thanks to their aromatherapeutic powers.

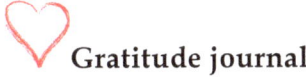
Gratitude journal

After releasing my emotions in the journal at bedtime, I then filled a page with the things I felt gratitude for that day. At one stage, I could see no good in my life. This process forced me to appreciate small things like my morning coffee, a smile, sunshine, green lights, birds singing, acts of kindness from strangers and big things like family, friends and every contact with Don from the other side.

This is now easy, and Don is always on the gratitude list I write every night. Self-care exercises hold immense value even when you are not grieving. It is of benefit to everyone.

 **Grounding**

This was one of the 'easy' ones I would do when I just needed to feel in control. When I thought, *'What can I do to feel better that isn't going to take much effort?'* as I had no energy or motivation. I would stand on the grass in the backyard with bare feet.

It was calming with minimum effort required. As instant gratification is the bane of our existence, please don't do this expecting to feel something like a sugar rush. It's calming, especially if you are in sunshine. This is to do with vibration. Science has proven that the minutest part of everything is a vibration of energy.

Our ancestors walked the earth in bare feet, but our lifestyle has placed barriers between our skin and the earth. Our feet are like a sponge that soaks up negatively charged electrons from the earth, so, when you don't feel safe, secure and stable, getting grounded with bare feet connected to nature is beneficial and easy.

Nobel Prize winner Richard Feynman has some interesting insights on this and claims that grounding equalises the electronic connection between our body and the earth, essentially making our body an extension of the earth's magnetic field. Huh? In a nutshell, an influx of negative electrons from the earth calms our nervous system by shifting us from a 'fight-or-flight' state to a 'rest-and-digest' state.

 **Journaling**

This was recommended by the grief counsellor and other practitioners.

When under stress before Don died, I would struggle to clear my mind before bed so I could get a good night's sleep.

It didn't matter if I couldn't sleep then because Don would be awake if I was (I think this was one of his superpowers). I wasn't alone.

After he died, the thought of being awake and alone in my grief in our bed all night terrified me. The 'before bed' regime included journaling and allowed me to empty my mind. I wrote as many pages as I needed to, to empty my emotions onto the page. Swearing was totally acceptable.

The journals I have filled to date are a testament to how difficult my journey through grief has been and have provided the invaluable 'look at how far I have come' indicator.

Laughing

"Always laugh when you can. It is cheap medicine." – Lord Byron

I found an effective way to raise my spirits was to watch comedy. I found I could laugh or at the very least smile by watching comedy on TV or YouTube whether I wanted to or not.

I watched *for as long as it took to feel the change in me*. To start with, this was difficult, and I think there was some guilt attached, but it progressively got easier to be okay with feeling lighter emotions. It's another self-care technique that is beneficial even when you're not grieving, and life just sucks!

Meditation

In the early stages of grieving I used guided meditations, and the most valuable was one where *I met with Don*. I cannot stress enough how important this one was to me at the beginning. It gave me a moment's peace. It still blows my mind that twenty-six months after Don died, the place I moved into was *the* room and outlook I had visualised more than twenty months earlier.

Follow your heart and know that whatever you choose to do is right. No one else's view on this is more important than yours. There is no letting go, there is just an element of acceptance.

Know that what you feel for this person does not go away. So, give yourself a break, and if you haven't tried a guided meditation before, please try it. The one I've recommended is a beautiful meditation that is easily accessible ('Coping with Grief' by Jason Stephenson). It was incredibly calming, and I played it before going to sleep. I always had a far better sleep afterwards.

I used at least one meditation a day, but usually one to start the day and one at the end. Another meditation YouTuber I enjoyed when I was *rebuilding myself* was Kenneth Soares. There is such a huge variety that I am sure you can find someone you like to listen to and hopefully create a habit. As a cheat on my deep breathing task, I would use breathing-based meditations, which were particularly beneficial at the beginning of my grieving.

I go to sleep every night with a sleep meditation running, although what I listen to varies with what I find I need at the time. There is so much available. I think my brain is so used to sleep meditations now that within a short time of the music/smooth talking starting, my brain says, *'Oh, sleep time'* and I'm almost immediately out of it.

 **Pets**

Although I questioned my decision to get a puppy *immediately after* he started using the house as a toilet, it was the right thing for me to do. I needed to be distracted, I needed company, I needed unconditional love, I needed to be needed, I needed more energy in the house. I needed to see life was fun and puppies are experts at finding fun in the inanest things.

This is exactly what I said about Don; he found fun in the inane. Both Don and Sparky had/have, respectively, a similar enthusiasm for life. Every time I wake and see his little face or when I come home to such love, it reinforces I could not have done this without him. The universe knew this, which is why Ralph came back. I know pets are not an option for everyone, but this was invaluable for me.

When I was pregnant with Stacey, I provided home care for an older woman who had terminal cancer. From diagnosis to passing was 7 weeks. Ironically, the value of me being there was significantly greater for her husband, and he kept me on after his wife's death for company. This arrangement couldn't continue as I was in the late stages of pregnancy but how could I leave him? Then I happened to rescue a kitten and it seemed the right thing to give the kitten to him. It was exactly what he needed, and I was able to leave them to it. This outcome was divinely guided, I am sure.

 **Photos**

Photos of Don are in virtually every room and on the lock and home screens on my devices. A couple of times I found the photos so deeply upsetting that I removed them for a few days.

I would look at earlier photos and think, '*I can't believe you left me,*' but the Don in that photo didn't leave me, it was an older version of Don that did. To gain perspective, I would periodically only look at recent ones to remind myself 'it was his time'.

It was harder to look at my face in the photos of both of us as it reminded me of how incredibly happy I was (past tense). I cannot deny, when looking at my face, what an incredible life I had with him. So, photos of Don are in my life every day and I change them when I need a different perspective.

I also have thirty-two photos chronicling our love spanning 1980–2017 in our anniversary video. Precious!

In a reading when Don had been gone 3 years, *he* told me to take all the photos out of the bedroom. I wouldn't have listened to anyone else on this. But the photos were enabling a ramp up of my grief every time I went to bed. By removing them, I opened a space where he could be closer to me and I was able to go to sleep feeling more at peace and without crying first.

 **Posture**

When grief takes over, there is comfort in the foetal position, but when you want to take control, holding a strong posture instead will increase your ability to fight through the pain.

Our body reflects our state of mind but it's a symbiotic relationship and we can change our state of mind by changing our posture. Hold yourself straight, raise your chin slightly upward, drop your shoulders down and back to open your chest and you will be surprised how strong that posture makes you feel.

On a smaller scale, if you hold a pencil between your teeth so it's poking out either side of your mouth, you can trick your mind into thinking you are smiling, and this can lighten your mood. Be patient, I have found it sometimes took a little while for my brain to register it was a smile.

♡ Relaxation

A hot bath with lavender oil, magnesium salts and baking soda while listening to relaxation music can be invaluable. I found, through the worst periods of grieving, that my whole body ached. Of course, this doesn't work so well in summer.

♡ Setting boundaries

There is so much vulnerability in the early stages of grieving. Everyone is different and personal preferences should be respected. If you don't feel strong enough to set boundaries, assign this to someone close. My daughter and son made sure my wishes were known. I was protected.

I didn't want to talk to anyone. They ensured that I wasn't handed a phone every time someone rang or that I wasn't dragged into conversations when people arrived.

I didn't want people dropping in on me, so I didn't stay at home on my own.

I chose not to see my husband's body carried out of our home. I didn't want that image in my head.

I set boundaries. What I couldn't enforce myself, my daughter or son supported me in – by ensuring people respected my wishes while I didn't have the strength to do so myself.

♡ Sleep

Studies have proven that lack of sleep can cause depression, so it's important to make sure you get this one under control.

I have a routine. I do a short salute to the sun yoga sequence if my body feels too tense to get into bed, then I journal to empty my mind, do my gratitude page to increase good endorphins, then I read while lying on a heat wheat. I put lavender oil on the soles of my feet. I take Nature's Own Complete Sleep tablets. If I still have trouble relaxing, I get onto the floor in the child's pose, with relaxation music playing, until the tension in my body dissolves. Finally, I go to sleep with a sleep meditation running. At times, I also have a hot milk drink.

For many years I have gone to sleep listening to a meditation so now my brain just switches off the moment the track starts and I'm asleep within minutes.

Quite often, I wake at 4am. Andy explained that my subconscious was still traumatised by Don dying beside me at 4am. Knowing there was a reason for this helped. It was understandable, therefore, it did not cause me stress.

Socialising

Don and I enjoyed being together to the extent that we rarely socialised much outside of family and a few friends. Because we had been together since I was eighteen, when Don died, loneliness was a major issue for me, as you would expect. I made a *commitment to myself* to accept any and all social offers from friends. This was *incredibly important*, and whether I wanted to or not, I never broke the commitment to myself.

Sound – Binaural beats

Binaural beats are similar to Solfeggio frequencies as they are about vibrations; however, with binaural beats a different frequency is played in each ear. This sound treatment requires headphones and is said to harness the brain's responsiveness to sound to move you into a state of deep relaxation, relieve anxiety, and help you sleep better.

I have also used these before for work stress, anxiety or when I have wanted to think more clearly.

Sound – Solfeggio frequencies

I personally have found this to be one of the easiest and quickest ways to improve my mood. There is so much available on the internet, and I pick what I need as the mood takes me, to relieve feelings of panic, sadness or to improve my concentration. I'll either play it with my eyes closed and relaxing or in the background while I'm doing something. A lot of research has been conducted on Solfeggio scales, which date back to the 11th Century; it's fascinating.

We already know from science that everything has a vibration and its own frequency. By subjecting the mind and body to a Solfeggio frequency, you can easily take on the balancing and healing properties of the frequency. There is research available that shows, for example that 528Hz has a stress-reducing effect on the endocrine system. It is worth looking into.

YouTube has countless Solfeggio meditations that integrate the frequencies with music – over a million pages were returned in a Google search on 'Solfeggio meditation'.

Talking out loud to Don

This was the single most important self-care I engaged in initially. I clearly saw when I was hurting and lashing out at Don or myself. It allowed me to monitor untruths, so they didn't fester, and I was shocked when I found I had entered the state of hopelessness. I googled feeling hopelessness and realised how close I was to ending it.

I knew everything I said was also heard by Don. He showed me this, multiple times, by responding to something I had said while I was in a reading.

If you have unspoken words for the person who has passed, it is not too late to mend a bridge, ask for explanations or forgiveness or get something off your chest.

I told Don the things I loved about him that had made losing him from my life so incredibly painful. I told him what I struggled with, like him leaving before our holiday, and I got closure on so many things.

I asked him who was going to do the dishes now (still waiting for an answer on that one).

Self-talk out loud is a magnificent clearing house. Most times it is spontaneous, unfiltered speech that speaks volumes on what is going on in your head.

 **Vibrations**

The basics of this has been proven by science but, in a nutshell, everything in this universe, including ourselves, is a vibration.

I am definitely at the beginning of a learning curve on vibrations, but I understand love is 528Hz here and on the other side. Grief is 75Hz, and low vibrations can cause illness. So, managing your grief, when you are able to, is really important.

People vibrating at a low frequency are more susceptible to disease and 'bad fortune' as these also vibrate at a low level.

Solfeggio scales are vibrations that heal because they are at a higher vibration, which help us raise our vibrations to a healthier one.

The same frequencies are attracted to each other. We attract and feel more comfortable with people on the same frequency as us. So, if you are angry, you will attract and feel a kinship to other angry people. Whereas, vibrating in a good space will attract kindness and good fortune. For me, this good vibration represents peace.

When you feel trapped in a low state of mind, and you recognise it as a low vibration, it is easier to seek the antidote of a higher vibration than to try to work through your emotions.

Try not to focus on the emotion and instead just deal with raising your vibration. This can be done by walking in nature, doing something you enjoy, laughing, smiling, feeling love from someone (I find children and animals are a ready source of the antidote).

If emotion has you feeling trapped and is getting in your way of doing any of those things, put in your ear, or in the background, 528Hz or 432Hz Solfeggio music. It will raise your spirits. I do this all the time, especially when I feel stuck in an unhappy space.

Walking in nature

I believe in the healing energy of nature, especially trees and water (even before I understood about vibrations). I know they have a calming effect on me, and I've been told that when I need to feel closer to Don to stand with my feet in the river or ocean.

I committed myself to regularly walking Sparky and found the most beautiful, serene dog park in my area full of gum trees and native birds. Sparky and I start and finish every day with a walk in the park. I never would have anticipated having this much exercise in my life, but it's easy with Sparky and it became addictive because it was always incredibly calming.

 **Water**

Drink plenty of water, especially if you are feeling anxious. Dehydration can increase your cortisol levels (stress hormones), while also producing the bodily sensations that feel like an anxiety attack. Research is available that shows even mild dehydration can influence your mood, energy levels and the ability to think clearly.

 **Writing without thinking**

This technique was recommended to me by a grief counsellor. It is hard because we don't write for long periods of time anymore (although I write in the journal every night) and my hand would get tired before I had exhausted what was in my mind. But it cleared so much out of my head that I wasn't aware I was thinking. This is not recommended as an ongoing practice but as a way to release emotion that is at a critical mass in your body.

 **Putting a 'wow' in my future**

I experienced a lot of lethargy in grief, and although I knew I needed to put something in my future that I would look forward to, it required unwavering determination to follow through on.

It was only my determination that stopped me from cancelling my wow holiday and giving up looking for Sparky, and the fact that I had a strong desire for these to eventuate. I know others who have cancelled their wow, through fear. It's a difficult time to venture out. It needs determination. Make it something you know will excite and ignite you (at some point). Tell people so you can't back out and you can use their enthusiasm to keep you moving. My wows were exactly what I wanted and needed.

Yoga

When I couldn't quieten my mind or handle the level of emotion in my body when I was trying to go to sleep, I would move onto the floor and take up the child pose. It helps release tension in the chest, back and shoulders and helps to reduce stress and anxiety. I would stay on the floor until I could feel all the anxiety had drained from my body, then I would go back to bed.

When I started to venture out on my own, I joined a yoga studio and paid for a full month to force myself to commit to regular yoga practice.

After I finished the month, I reverted to doing the salute to the sun sequence while waiting for my heat wheats to heat up in preparation for bed.

My regularly broken promise to myself is to do more yoga. I will do better on this, I promise.

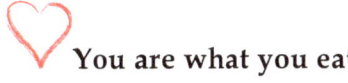
You are what you eat

Nutrition has always been important to me, and I was intrigued when I was advised by the nutritionist to eat more green foods because this is the best food group for the heart. It aligns with the colour of the heart chakra.

In addition, sunshine, mangos and pineapples are good for depression as yellow is the colour of the solar plexus chakra. It's interesting learning about this. Yellow foods are mood enhancers and I have always said our Queensland mangos (which can be used in both yellow and orange groups) is like eating sunshine.

Naturally, eating from every food colour is optimal, but in situations like grief, increasing your green foods will be beneficial. Examples of colour groups are:

- ♥ *Root chakra* (red) includes strawberries, tomato, red meat and turmeric.
- ♥ *Sacral chakra* (orange) includes carrots, mangos, salmon and cinnamon.
- ♥ *Solar plexus chakra* (yellow) includes pineapple, corn, lemons and yellow curries.
- ♥ *Heart chakra* (green) includes spinach, green apples, green tea and spirulina.
- ♥ *Throat chakra* (blue) includes blueberries, blackberries and herbal tea.
- ♥ *Third eye chakra* (indigo) includes purple grapes, eggplants and blueberries.
- ♥ *Crown chakra* includes fasting and detoxing.

'I need help' self-care

Note: This list is of self-care opportunities that involve others and is alphabetical; you need to rate each item's importance to you.

 Clairvoyance/readings

This book is evidence of how important this one was for me. It gave me a greater understanding of where/what Don was now and it gave me perspective on why I was where I was.

The guy that was my rock was still my rock, and when I needed to hear what he had to say, I did.

Loneliness is the biggest challenge I faced. I know I was never alone, but I still experienced loneliness often. I wanted my conversations with Don to be two-way. I used readings to give me an anchor and a connection to Don that I wouldn't have had on my own.

Don's exit from my life was sudden and unexpected. These readings gave me the space and time I needed to gradually reduce my dependence on his presence in my life.

Through readings, I have continued to receive precious words of love and understanding.

 Creative outlets – art therapy

I was told that being creative would help me and I (accidentally) found art therapy sessions when the universe decided this is what I needed. These proved to be incredibly relaxing and therapeutic. It doesn't require artistic talents; it's an expression of emotion through the creative process with a trained art therapist. I enjoyed this so much that I went every week for five months and only stopped because the evening sessions were no longer offered. At this time in my grieving, it was my only out-of-home activity as it was before my dog park walks started.

 Creative outlets – your passion

There are many ways to express creativity, and I truly believe its benefits come, in part, because you are using the part of your brain that is not trying to work everything out and put logic behind it. Give your brain a break! Find your creative outlet or *passion*, whether it be music or sewing, gardening, art, pottery, woodworking or anything.

 Energy healing - kinesiology

A form of energy healing, kinesiology was recommended by a trusted friend. I engaged in this treatment in the first year of life without Don. The practice uses muscle testing to detect and correct imbalances that may relate to stress. The kinesiologist was superb and helped me understand how I was processing the grief and the effect it was having on my body.

As part of the treatment I was given aromatherapy essential oil 'Joy', which was serendipitous because finding joy resonated with me; it's also my middle name and the fragrance *was* uplifting.

 Energy healing - emotion and body code

A form of energy healing new to me, but it was highly recommended. It was an insightful experience as it clears stuff on a level we couldn't reach and provides clarity on the cause of the pain.

Naturally my first session was around grief because I was consumed by it, so Cara removed the unhealthy element of emotions related to Don's death including the shock my body and mind suffered.

She also removed two cords from when I was forty-six, this is when I had terminated the pregnancy. Plus, I had (understandably) added crying and guilt to my emotional baggage post Don's death. And it is baggage. When this was all released, I felt lighter. That was the decider for me. I felt better with no effort on my part but an understanding of how my thoughts weigh me down so, four years after Don died, this is my main form of healing/treatment.

 Energy healing – massages

In addition to relaxing muscles, massage is also known to reduce stress hormones. My naturopath advised that massages would be therapeutic as having hands on me would help me feel.

"One of the immediate benefits of massage is a feeling of deep relaxation and calm. This occurs because massage prompts the release of endorphins – the brain chemicals (neurotransmitters) that produce feelings of wellbeing. Levels of stress hormones, such as adrenaline, cortisol and norepinephrine, are also reduced." (Source: www.betterhealth.vic.gov.au/health)

 Energy healing – reiki

I used various reiki practitioners during this time. Other than feeling lighter and clearer mentally afterwards, I also experienced significant relief from the tightness in my abdomen and chest, which is where my grief was accumulating.

 Grief counsellor

This was an invaluable service that enabled me to talk about Don without someone trying to make me feel better, as friends and family invariably did. I spoke easily without fear of judgement.

I loved being able to talk about Don. This was uplifting, and I felt closer to Don when I was talking about him. My first counsellor got me, understood my loss and helped me. The second one was lovely but not as helpful as the first one.

I was given exercises that proved invaluable in processing my thoughts and understanding the process, including journaling my thoughts and keeping a gratitude journal. Both exercises have become part of my 'normal' life. The second counsellor gave me the writing without thinking exercise, which proved beneficial at the time.

The most important element here is to make sure you resonate on some level with the counsellor. If not, change to another counsellor.

 Nutritionists

Stress consumes great quantities of vitamins and minerals that are generated or stored in your body. It is essential to your health to replenish these until, at the least, you feel you don't need them anymore. For a couple of years, I had been seeing a nutritionist who was replenishing what I was losing through work stress. The first day I took the supplements I could not believe how much clearer my mind was and that my energy levels survived to the end of the day.

Following Don's death, the supplements were aligned to specifically what grief depletes from the body. As time moved on the supplements changed, and I was managing my nutrient intake largely through diet. I continue to take magnesium and vitamin B.

Don was a big fan of taking vitamin B every day and more when life was stressful. He gave many family and friends a bottle of vitamin B when they were going through a stressful time. After he died, I put his large bottle of vitamin B tablets next to his photo on his side of the bed. This is where I felt his presence the strongest. I could hear him telling me to take vitamin B. On occasion, I would say to him (as I did prior to his death), "No, I only need one today," and I took at least one every day.

> You cannot solve a problem with the same mind that created it.
>
> Unknown

31
You are who you think you are – still

I don't try to make life fit my beliefs; my beliefs are written in pencil and are always open to editing when a new understanding flows into my life that resonates.

The following is an update to the list of beliefs we had when Don died (Part I, Chapter 3). I have learned so much but will never assume I know it all, so this is still always ready for edits and additions.

- We knew you could connect and communicate with passed people and spirit guides because we had both experienced this. Updates:

  - ♥ We can communicate through mediums after a recently deceased person has completed healing, although how long that takes is based on the individual. If you can't connect, you are not meant to *yet*, so try again later.

  - ♥ After healing, they can communicate directly with us more easily within the first three months, although from my experience that varies. After the three months, we need to have a clearer, happier vibration to reach them as they can't get through thick, negative energy we live in.

  - ♥ We can only communicate with people who have passed who are willing and able to communicate with us. We can, however, always communicate with our spirit guides.

- ♥ It is my understanding that we all have the ability to communicate with the other side to varying degrees, although some come with the skill as part of their life plan. Social conditioning is often what creates the barrier to communicating. Step 1: Be open. It is my view that our intuition is messages from our own higher self, the part of us still connected to the other side.

♡ We are a soul (eternal) having a human (mortal) experience.

- ♥ My view on this is unchanged at this stage, and Don, now the eternal soul in this relationship, has not given any indication to the contrary.

♡ God/s, Source, Higher Power, Universe, Buddha, etc. are the same energy that is interpreted differently by people, religions, cultures (referred to in this book as *Higher Power et al.*)

- ♥ *Higher Power et al.* is not an entity, it is everything. It is the energy that is everything in the universe and here on Earth, including ourselves. *"God is not He who is, but That which is."* – Philosopher Baruch Spinoza.

♡ Our human existence (aka life) is for learning and growth. It's not a holiday, it's a classroom. So, don't expect every day to be sunny and spent on the beach. Challenges are not something going wrong, they are the lessons we are here to learn from.

- ♥ My view on this is unchanged at this stage.

♡ Love is the only thing that survives and is the glue in our life purpose.

♥ My view on this is unchanged at this stage.

♡ We reincarnate. Don and I knew, without knowing specifics, that we'd had many previous lives together.

♥ We choose to reincarnate; some souls choose not to.

♥ We bring gifts and baggage from previous lives. The baggage is brought here so our soul can grow through learning.

♥ Gifts and baggage – think prodigies and unexplained phobias as well as instant connections, good or bad, with someone you just met.

♥ People who can suddenly speak a foreign language they have never learned (in this lifetime) are tapping into a previous life.

♥ Clues to your previous lives can be revealed in what you are passionate about and what you have an unexplained aversion to.

♥ If you want to truly understand yourself, look into your past lives. I had no idea, before Don died, the extent to which our past lives influenced us in this one.

♥ We reincarnate with people (and sometimes animals) from our soul family. These are usually partners and friends and explains why our connection to them is sometimes closer than family. They are here to help us as we are them.

♥ We bring wisdom as well as pain to heal from our previous lives. We are more complex than we can comprehend with our human brain and the ten percent of that which we use.

♡ We plan our lives before we get here with challenges to overcome. If you ignore the lesson of a challenge it will repeat until you get it.

♥ A roadmap to our life plan and the challenges we came to overcome are in our birth number.

♥ Our life plan is on GPS. If you make a decision that takes you 'off your path', your journey will adjust. If you are not ready for a fork in the road, your journey will adjust. The opportunity will appear when you are ready. You are never not on your path. (I sold our house two years after Don died, not six months, which was the original universe plan.) Don told me, "You are on your path, no matter what path you are on."

♡ We learn through change and new experiences. That's why these two things are a constant in our life.

♥ There are no mistakes, only lessons to learn.

♥ People come into your life for a reason. Some to help you gain more knowledge and understanding, others to provide a challenge you are here to learn from.

♥ Your life and your choices are 100 percent yours.

♥ Meeting Don, building a strong, unbreakable, loving relationship and then losing him was part of my life plan (sucks to be me). But this was

- essential because this book was also part of my plan.
- ♥ Everything you need to know you downloaded and brought with you. You just need to look within.
- ♥ If you ignore the lesson of a challenge it will repeat until you get it. (Repeated because it's an important one to understand, and my life really changed when I understood this one.)
- ♡ We plan our exits, which may be in the form of illness or accident, sudden or prolonged. There are no accidental deaths.
  - ♥ It has been said that we place five potential exit points in our life plan.
  - ♥ We only die when the soul leaves the body. You cannot leave this life if it is not your soul's plan to do so. There are no accidental deaths.
  - ♥ We leave this life as per our plan, and old age is not written into everyone's life plan.
  - ♥ Some souls are here for a short time as their plan is purely to be of service in one of their soul family's life plan (i.e. children/babies who die young).
- ♡ Don and I do not believe in Hell, except the one some people make for themselves in this life. The concept of Hell is a dominant premise in religions and can be seen as a means to control through fear and judgement.
  - ♥ We are here to learn from our mistakes, not be dammed by them.

- ♥ When you believe in reincarnation, you understand there is no-one left to go to hell. We all come home.

- ♥ I don't know if the devil exists, but I know there is evil in the world. It has been written that people who are truly evil do not 'go home'. One book says they immediately re-enter this world as a baby. Another book says they come back as a victim.

- ♡ We didn't have a clear view on Heaven except we know there is a place we go to between lives. But if religions invented Hell, what did that mean for Heaven?

- ♥ We ALL go HOME.

- ♥ We are all welcomed when we return home. Nobody is denied access!

- ♥ Nothing you do here will stop you from going home. The worst scenario I think is that you're just going home with more baggage and lessons to learn than you planned. And with a lot of healing to do on the other side.

- ♡ Judgement. Nope, not buying it. *Higher Power et al.* is love – that's it. Judgement is ego-based. Ego is a trait of human beings, not higher beings. Spirituality is absence of ego.

- ♥ We plan our lives and the lessons before we incarnate, then review our life against our plan when we return.

- ♥ The 'judgment' that occurs is our own self-review with our guides and teachers, and is part of the healing process.

- ♥ The review is specific to all *emotionally charged situations* in our life, good and bad.

- ♥ There is an understanding that everyone does the best they can with the information/abilities they have at that time. Therefore, the only outcome from a negative emotional experience is lessons learned.

- ♥ It is my understanding, but written in pencil, that learning your lesson (for more serious situations) may require you to come back in your next life on the opposite side of a situation you created before (i.e. people who do harm may come back next time as a victim; a racist may come back next time in a minority group).

- ♥ It's unfair to judge people because you have no idea what their back stories are or the challenges they set themselves for this life.

Change your thoughts and you change your world.

Normal Vincent Peale

Conclusion: From our hearts to yours

When I started to write this book, I wanted to help people navigate deep, debilitating grief by recounting my experience. Generally, there is an incredible amount of love and support available from family, friends and community; however, I have absolutely no doubt that Don was integral to my healing and that his involvement was to provide me with an experience with death and grief that would be told in this book. This is what makes my story mine and I appreciate one of us had to remain here for the book to be written. Don is so entrenched in my story, that it's ours.

I also have a new appreciation for the part I played in my own healing. Everything happened for a reason. Everything happened *for* me.

As with everyone else, I know people who are 'on the clock' and live every day with an awareness of impending death. Then there are those that go without warning. And there is also an increasingly older generation who know they have more years behind them than ahead. And, understandably, mainly because of upbringing and culture, there are so many people who fear death.

Please understand, our only intention is to tell our story and for people to take from it what resonates. I am not pushing my beliefs onto you. You are as free to choose what you believe as I am.

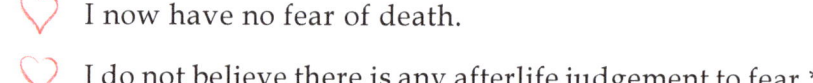

What did I gain from my experience?

- I now have no fear of death.
- I do not believe there is any afterlife judgement to fear.*
- I know I'm going 'home' when I die.
- I know Don will be there to meet me.
- I know death will free me from any pain and suffering present here, in this life.
- I know death will *not* separate me from those I leave behind (this is important).
- I have a far greater appreciation of life that comes from a better understanding of death.

(*except *our own* review of whether we learned what we planned to in this life. The review is on highly emotive events, both blessings and lessons.)

Conclusion: from our hearts to yours

My perspective on living as someone still on this side of death is as follows:

- **Baggage** – I will consciously work to let go of any anger, resentment, guilt or regret that comes into my life. It serves no purpose for me to carry it and its absence will help me enjoy the life I have, *while I have it*. I choose to let go. This, to me, guides my attitude.

- **Acceptance** – Don and I knew we were connected at soul level and that the soul survived death. I accept that in death only the body dies. I accept everything happens *for* us, not *to* us. If I look, I *will* find the good in every experience. This, to me, guides my gratitude.

The suffering I was to experience was planned. I brought with me pain of separation from Don in two previous lives and I'm sure this is why he promised to never leave me.

This is my story. Therefore, for me to be able to reconnect with Don after his death is beyond words! Ironically, the person who could help ease my suffering was also the person who created it, but I cannot imagine having to go through this without him. It's fitting for us that he supported me through my grief.

Knowing your loved one has gone to a good place may be all the comfort you are looking for, from them. Grief is about you, no-one else.

And, most importantly, **everyone's journey is different.** Everyone has a different experience of grief. *Our* story potentially started in the 1700s and I believe that what transpired for me/us was what had to happen for this book to be written, and, as Don advised me several times, I would be speaking my truth.

I don't know what your story will be, but you do have a unique story that will be one of survival.

I believe the connection and communication I have with Don is 5G. Some may also have this connection while some could be on cups and string, dial-up or something else entirely.

I think your level of acceptance of life after death, and the age of your soul, all impact your 'after-death' experience. But I am surmising as I only really know what happened to us.

If you haven't had a psychic reading before, *and want to try it*, approach it in an open mind and a light-hearted manner. We once went with a group of friends to a psychic fair 'for a laugh'. No pressure. Everyone enjoyed it. All readings were private, and you shared what you wanted to. Interestingly, my reader at this fair told me I had three children. She was including in the count, my terminated pregnancy when I was forty-six. Indeed, the baby I didn't have is still a part of me, as was evidenced in a line on my palm, and now that soul is here as my beautiful granddaughter.

Most importantly for me is that I know after *I go*, my children and grandchildren and maybe even great grandchildren, will expect flickering lights, butterflies and birds and feathers, and I will be giving them and everyone I know messages of love from the other side.

from Don's heart to yours...

Don was one of life's characters, and he would tell you with relish, *he survived death!*

Don had inadvertently prepared himself for his death and successfully closed off the final chapter of the character he was.

Conclusion: from our hearts to yours

The following are extracts from this book specific to information on what Don experienced after he died and are insights on where he is. I hope Don's experience, expressed in my words, can provide anyone with a fear of death an alternative perspective that brings a sense of understanding and peace.

From Part II, Chapter 6:

 He let me know he was now in a good place, free of fear and pain.

From Part II, Chapter 11:

 Even after death, Don was behaving the same, doing the sorts of things he would have had he been alive. It seemed irrefutable that it was only his body that had died. 'Don' was not his body; he was still here, and he was still Don (The first of many examples of this was when he introduced me to his grandfather, Ernest).

From Part II, Chapter 15:

 Don revealed he had an element of control over how and when he went and why he made the choices he did. He didn't have an option not to die but he decided he didn't want to die away from me, away from home, on his birthday or in a hospital. *So, he didn't!*

 Don said, "I'm happy. I feel like freedom. I can go wherever I want. It is freedom."

 Rouna said he didn't have to take *anything* (negative emotions) with him. She said that with some people she saw *it took them weeks or months because they took so much anger and hatred from this world so that they didn't*

heal easily. There was nothing like that with Don. He was a free spirit; he was good.

♡ *"It's about the heart, it's got nothing to do with time."* (Quote from Don on grieving duration.)

♡ *"Understand where this (psychic) connection comes from; it's supposed to come from the heart – a soul connection."* (Beware of psychics where it's like they are just reading from a book.)

From Part II, Chapter 18:

♡ Don said he'd gone *home! This message was a gift from Don.* We couldn't get a better destination. Everyone gets to go HOME when they die. Whew!

♡ Don also recommended the following books, and you can't get any higher recommendation than to have a book *on* the other side endorsed from the other side. The books are:

- ♥ *Life on the Other Side* by Sylvia Browne
- ♥ *Journey of Souls* by Michael Newton
- ♥ *Talking to Heaven* by James van Praagh

From Part II, Chapter 25:

♡ *"I did learn a lot in that lifetime; some of it was lessons, some blessings."* (About his last life, but really it's about life.)

♡ *"This is part of her journey and she chose it anyway."* (Reminding me it was part of the blueprint *I* created for my journey.)

Conclusion: from our hearts to yours

♡ *"When your time comes, he will be there to show you the way over. He says, 'I love you, but I don't want you to be here. I know you have so much to do."* (a reminder I have so much more to do in my life and that we are all here for a purpose)

♡ *"'till death do us part' – who made up those words because that's not true. We didn't part!"* (Don's posthumous humorous view on marriage vows.)

♡ Annette's points in this reading to provide some clarity on what to expect:

- ♥ After about three months they shift to a higher vibration where they won't be seeing everything we do.
- ♥ Then a thought will bring a loved one closer. Imagine they are in another room that we can't come into until we've passed over. The entrance to that room comes closer to us. But a thought will bring them through.
- ♥ They will also come on special occasions, and it will be easier for them as it won't be the thick dense energy of us needing them to be there.

From Part II, Chapter 26:

♡ Don said, *"I know you are going to be okay. You can see a lot clearer from over here what is going on."*

♡ He also said, *"Know and believe that there is more going on than we can see down there."*

♡ He said, *"We were so devoted to each other and that emotion doesn't go anywhere, it's still here."* (You don't stop loving people because their body died; it's just not possible.)

♡ *"They have you walking over a swing bridge and swaying from side to side."* Don said, *"It's okay, we've needed to shake you up sometimes to get the emotions and crying out but it's going to straighten up for you."* (Everything happens for a reason, especially the uncomfortable episodes)

Resources that have helped shape my views

Books

Albom, Mitch (1997): *Tuesdays with Morrie*

Browne, Sylvia (2000, July 17): *Life on the Other Side*

Chopra, Deepak (2006, October 17): *Life After Death*

Hay, Louise (1984, January 1): *You Can Heal Your Life*

Millman, Dan (1995, April 11): *The Life You Were Born to Live*

Newton, Michael (1994, November 29): *Journey of Souls*

Schwartz, Robert (2012, November 2): *The Soul's Gift*

Spiller, Jan (1997, November 1): *Astrology for the Soul*

van Praagh, James (1997, November 1): *Talking to Heaven*

Weiss, Brian L, MD (1988, September 1): *Many Lives, Many Masters*

Psychics

Cara Jade Green: Cara combines personal spirituality, ancient wisdom, kinesiology, energy healing, emotion code and body code and shamanic healing.
@carajadegreen (FB)
carajadegreen@outlook.com

Rouna Faraj: Rouna is a Psychic/Medium who has the gifts of clairvoyance, clairaudience and psychometry.
rouna@mediumrouna.com.au
www.mediumrouna.com.au

Melanie Crawford: Melanie is a clairvoyant medium who combines mediumship and channelled healings.
@melanie.crawford.clairvoyant,
https://melanie-crawford.com/
melaniecrawford333@gmail.com

YouTube Healers I personally recommend:

Jason Stephenson: Sleep Mediation Music
'Coping with Grief' meditation
Reclaim the power within. Tribute to Robin Williams

Kenneth Soares: I recommend so many of Kenneth's as he incorporates healing vibrations helpful for sleep and to free your busy mind.
Guided mediation 432Hz Let go, Deep Healing, Connect with Soul tribe
Guided Sleep Mediation 432 Hz Enhance Self-Love, Patience, Joy and Positive Energy

Resources that have helped shape my views

Volunteering

Elephant Nature Park http://www.elephantnaturepark.org/

The Elephant rescue and rehabilitation center in Thailand is where you can volunteer to help. Volunteers and visitors contribute to the healing while learning about the elephants lives past and present.

Elephant Nature Park – Dog Project

https://www.saveelephant.org/dogproject/

While at the Elephant Park, volunteers can also help in the dog project which includes walking dogs recovering from surgery and just spending time with the dogs so they have regular human contact that is filled with love and care.

Acknowledgments

I will be eternally grateful to Don, for giving me everything I needed from him and more in this life. It was an incredible ride. And with equal enthusiasm I thank posthumous Don, who continues to watch over me, guide me, love me, support me and make me laugh. I am forever yours.

I am incredibly grateful to my children, who recognised that the incredible love I have for their father did not diminish the love I have for them. When their father died, they lost their mother for a very long time. They looked out for me. I know this. You are two of the most caring, wonderful people on this Earth, and we are so proud of you.

I am incredibly grateful to Sparky for absorbing so much of my grief and loving me anyway. Thank you for coming back for me.

To my granddaughters Lilliana, you are a precious blessing that melted my heart so I could feel love again and for Delilah, you bring so much joy, my heart overflows.

A special thank you to Melanie, Andy, Annette, Cara, Rouna and Moira. All of these gifted people helped bridge the gap between Don and I after he left this world. Your gift and presence in my life was exactly what I needed. You are all in my life as blessings. Thank you.

I am indebted to Lek and the Elephant Nature Park for gracing the world with one of the purest caring and compassionate

Acknowledgments

places on earth. You helped open my heart so the healing could take hold. Thank you

And to absolutely everyone who has ever been in my life, I would like you to know your presence was and is treasured. Whether you were in my life as lessons or blessings, I understand I met you for a reason and we did good! And for those I am yet to meet, *I'm ready!*

www.ingramcontent.com/pod-product-compliance
Lightning Source LLC
Chambersburg PA
CBHW040239010526
44107CB00065B/2807